EARLY CHILDHOOD EDUCATION SERIES

Sharon Ryan, *Editor*

Continued

Early Childhood Education Series, *continued*

Leading Anti-Bias Early Childhood Programs

—A GUIDE FOR CHANGE—

Louise Derman-Sparks
Debbie LeeKeenan
John Nimmo

Foreword by Mariana Souto-Manning

Teachers College
Columbia University
New York and London

National Association for the Education
of Young Children
Washington DC

Published simultaneously by Teachers College Press, 1234 Amsterdam Avenue, New York, NY 10027 and and the National Association for the Education of Young Children, 1313 L Street NW, Suite 500, Washington, DC 20005

Library of Congress Cataloging-in-Publication Data can be obtained at www.loc.gov

ISBN 978-0-8077- 5598-3 (paper)
ISBN 978-0-8077-7340-6 (ebook)

NAEYC item #7229

Printed on acid-free paper

Manufactured in the United States of America

22   21   20   19   18   17   16   15   8   7   6   5   4   3   2   1

Contents

Foreword

Injustice anywhere is a threat to justice everywhere.

—Rev. Martin Luther King Jr.

Anti-bias education is a critical approach to teaching and learning that recognizes that change is needed. Anti-bias educators actively challenge prejudices and injustices. They engage in critical thinking and problem solving, supporting all children in developing a fuller understanding of themselves and their place in the world. Anti-bias teaching helps children strengthen their identities as capable and empowered human beings. Through anti-bias education, young children identify issues and inequities in their lives, ask questions, consider multiple perspectives, and think about their lives critically, growing to actively resist prejudice and discrimination. Anti-bias education acknowledges that while education is a human right, in today's classrooms, schools, and society, biases are shaping the experiences and very futures of young children.

While some may think that the United States is a postracial society since the election of President Barack Obama or that there is no need to engage in this kind of work, we must consider the larger context of today's society. Social, racial, and cultural injustice is, unfortunately, all too common for many people, including People of Color, immigrants, and individuals with disabilities. This larger context shapes the worlds and experiences of young children today. So as educators, we must read the world critically and engage in challenging injustices. In doing so, we can rewrite what is and envision a new, hopeful, and just tomorrow.

Recognizing the need for anti-bias education to transcend the walls of individual classrooms, Louise Derman-Sparks, Debbie LeeKeenan, and John Nimmo invite early childhood program leaders to engage in this work as an imperative. Acknowledging that social, racial, and cultural justice ideas and values continue to be controversial to many, *Leading Anti-Bias Early Childhood Programs: A Guide for Change* addresses the following questions:

- What is the role of a leader in building anti-bias programs?
- As leaders, how do we build and/or grow anti-bias early childhood programs?

In this wonderful book, Louise, Debbie, and John conceptualize anti-bias work as a journey and acknowledge that we all start in different locations. Instead of seeing these different starting points as obstacles or problems, they offer multiple pathways to anti-bias leadership, which foster anti-bias teaching and learning. They invite you to journey through a variety of settings that illustrate how anti-bias education leaders

must keep their eye on the journey as well as the destination. While the urgency to do anti-bias education is great, the process of change happens over time. A slow, continuous process supports real human growth and builds skills and a committed school culture.

This process becomes accessible as readers embark on a learning journey though the pages of this book.

Through a variety of examples, invitations, and suggestions on addressing challenges in productive ways, Louise, Debbie, and John invite us to practice what they teach—that we need to recognize differences as diversities and not as deficits; that we must acknowledge how differences are positive, eliminating our own biases. Yet they posit that it is not enough to engage in non-bias education and leadership; early educators must take activist stances, engaging in anti-bias teaching, learning, and leadership.

Leading Anti-Bias Early Childhood Programs: A Guide for Change offers a clear conceptual framework, useful strategies, and practical tools for early childhood leaders—novice and experienced—who are starting or deepening their anti-bias approach to leading early childhood programs. Having early childhood program leaders as the primary audience, this book builds on the work of anti-bias education and features the authors' varied experiences as early childhood program directors in distinct settings. Considering conflict and tension as indicators of change, but acknowledging the challenges inherent in such processes, the authors guide early childhood program leaders to create communities that not only acknowledge and support differences, but also have a climate where conflict, risk-taking, and discomfort are positively supported and expected as inherent processes for living and working in a diverse world that affirms diversities.

Making anti-bias leadership real, the book features individuals with experience leading effective early childhood anti-bias education programs that serve diverse populations. The scenarios, suggestions, strategies, and examples presented are based on knowledge grounded in experiences. Through vivid examples, the authors recognize that anti-bias work involves not only working with teachers and their teaching, but also policies, procedures, admissions, budget, and hiring. In a practical and accessible way, the book features many tools that can be immediately employed by early childhood leaders. Examples of such tools include: (1) critical questions about the program learning environment that can aid leaders to document what *is* in order to envision possibilities and set goals; (2) interview questions that can aid the teacher hiring process; and (3) activities fostering the transformation of early childhood teachers and teaching.

This is an essential book for administrators, leaders, and directors in early educational settings; it is a book for all who work with early childhood teachers in mentoring, supervisory, or development roles. In reading this book, you will be invited to engage, question, reflect, act and transform not only your program, but also yourself as a leader! Whether you have teachers who are mentoring others in anti-bias teaching, teachers who are learning, teachers who are beginning the journey, teachers who are resistant to engage in this work, or teachers who may be uncomfortable acknowledging and talking about diversities, this book has something valuable and insightful for you.

Leading Anti-Bias Early Childhood Programs: A Guide for Change informs any leader's role in building and sustaining anti-bias early childhood programs in powerful ways, and in doing so it inspires leaders to stand up, get started, transform, and envision more hopeful and just possibilities with teachers, staff, families, allies, and stakeholders on behalf of our youngest children. As we readers consider the invitations issued in this book—most importantly, to actively engage in anti-bias leadership and to speak up for social and cultural justice—may we move beyond the comfort of what is familiar and remember that, as Martin Luther King Jr. said, "Our lives begin to end the day we become silent about things that matter."

Mariana Souto-Manning

Acknowledgments

Anti-bias education is a journey. So, too, is writing collaboratively. As with anti-bias work, it involves hard work, learning from and with each other, sometimes needing to find the third space to resolve different perspectives on an issue, and, always, moving forward.

Much of this book is based on the experiences of Debbie LeeKeenan, as director of the Eliot–Pearson Children's School at Tufts University from 1996 to 2013, and of John Nimmo, as executive director of the Child Study and Development Center at the University of New Hampshire from 2003 to 2013. We recognize and extend our immense gratitude to all the staff, teachers, families, and children who attended the programs during that time. Thank you for all the questions, insights, learning, and love over the years. In addition, our colleagues in the Eliot–Pearson Department of Child Study and Human Development at Tufts University and the Department of Human Development and Family Studies at University of New Hampshire provided support for our work.

Together, we thank Marie Ellen Larcada, our unflappable editor at Teachers College Press, who showed us much appreciated patience, guidance, encouragement, and humor from the inception to the completion of this book. We also are indebted to the tireless and generous work of Susan Liddicoat, who edited the first draft with precision, understanding, and care, and for the helpful suggestions and efforts of the publications and marketing staff at the Press. Our heartfelt appreciation also to our many colleagues who contributed to the ideas in this book: Dora Chen, Catherine Goins, Luis Hernandez, Eric Hoffmann, Peter Mangione, Mary Pat Martin, Patty Ramsey, and Ellen Wolpert.

Debbie LeeKeenan: I would like to recognize these individual teachers, at the Eliot–Pearson Children's School—Heidi Given, David Robinson, Lisa Kuh, Maryann O'Brien, Betty Allen, Chris Bucco, Maggie Beneke, Ben Mardell, Iris Ponte, Caryn Park, and Yvonne Liu-Constant—for their particular contributions, conversations, and inspirations about anti-bias education. I acknowledge two parent leaders who also contributed greatly to the anti-bias work—Vonda Wright and Eleanor Catino. The whole is greater than the sum of its parts. Thank you for the synergy.

John Nimmo: At the Child Study and Development Center, I am particularly indebted to staff members on the Diversity, Equity, and Bias Taskforce (DEBT) and Special Rights Taskforce who challenged me with their honesty, energy, and commitment. Specific appreciation goes to Pam Battin-Sacks, Nicole Cavicchi, Sandy Cormier, Laurie Conrad, Karen DuBois-Garofalo, Elizabeth Felder, Beth Gachowski, Allison Panneton Gray, Karen Juall, Sarah Leonard, Soyean Park, Lisa Pollaro, Harlee Tuttle, and Sara West. To CSDC parents, Heather Madore, Shannon Marthouse, and Vilmarie Sanchez, and to UNH colleagues, Bruce Mallory, Richard Haynes, Sean McGhee, and Wanda Mitchell, your courage and generosity made change seem and become possible.

Louise Derman-Sparks: I send heartfelt thanks to the many colleagues in the United States and internationally with whom I have worked over so many years. I am indebted to all of you for deepening and expanding my understanding of what diversity and equity work means—what differs contextually and what we hold in common. A special shout-out to Julie Olsen Edwards, who has been my steadfast soul sister and colleague for many, many years. I also acknowledge my debt to the friends who have stood by me through the vicissitudes of writing a book—in particular Catherine Goins, King Riley, Susan Phillips, Sue Romo, Ruth Tavlin, and Jen Ranger, my fabulous mountain dulcimer teacher, who understood missed sessions, weeks with no practice, and the value of music for keeping it together!

Our families supported us in big and small ways. I (Debbie) thank my husband Chris for taking this journey of being my life partner in the joys and challenges of being a multiracial family. Thank you for your love and support. To my children, Jason and Kira, and my granddaughter, Tabatha, I send my love and thank you for being my inspiration and motivation to do this work. I (John) hug my partner Shelly, who was with me on the anti-bias journey at our alma mater, Pacific Oaks College, almost 30 years ago and continues to amaze me today as she collaborates with refugee and immigrant communities. To our children, Ella and Jack, I send my love for the optimism and hope they give me for the next generation. I (Louise), as always, thank Bill, Doug, and Holly for their lifetime support.

Finally, we, Debbie and John, extend our deep appreciation to our mentor, Louise. Her vision and wisdom inspired us to lead anti-bias efforts in our programs and to embark on this journey of documentation.

Introduction

Our hope for creative living in this world house that we have inherited lies in our ability to reestablish the moral ends of our lives in personal character and social justice.

—Martin Luther King Jr. (1983, p. 58)

In this book we offer a conceptual framework, strategies, and practical tools for leaders who are initiating and growing anti-bias early childhood programs. The book builds upon the solid foundation laid by current thinking about best early childhood leader practices, while expanding them to incorporate the specific requirements of anti-bias education work. Our own experiences in building and leading successful anti-bias education programs and in working with leaders and teachers in the United States and other countries ground our writing.

Although we are aware of the many resources available for early childhood teachers seeking to introduce anti-bias education in their classrooms, there is little on the complex work of the leaders who set the stage for this approach. Together, we wrote this book for anyone who is already familiar with anti-bias education and wants to learn about what it takes to be an anti-bias leader of early childhood care and education programs (ECCE). This includes directors, managers, administrators, principals, and administrators of agencies—everyone who supervises early childhood programs. It will also be useful to the people who educate teachers and school leaders, including college faculty, teacher trainers, and coaches/mentors, as well as individual teachers who want to understand what creating an anti-bias program involves.

What our book does *not* address is how to implement anti-bias education with young children. To expand your understanding of what it means to integrate an anti-bias approach into the children's learning environment and curriculum, we refer you to several books that directly explore that subject (see Appendix A, available at www.tcpress.com, for self-study resources).

ORGANIZATION OF THIS BOOK

We have found that developing programs based on anti-bias education principles is a multifaceted undertaking requiring both organizational and educational change. It is doable—but only with persistence, time, and strategic thinking. Those realities are reflected in the content of this book.

Chapter 1 lays out key concepts that underlie the building of anti-bias ECCE programs. Chapter 2 reviews current research and thinking about the best practices for early childhood program leaders. It also notes how these practices set a foundation for effective anti-bias leadership. Chapter 3 explores the work of "reading the program" as an essential prelude to commencing strategic anti-bias education leadership. It describes relevant information to collect, provides tools for making sense of what you find, and suggests some basic preparatory steps. Chapters 4 and 5 discuss specific issues and strategies for working with staff and families. Chapter 6 builds on the themes of these two chapters, with professional development strategies for integrating, deepening, and sustaining anti-bias work after staff have come to understand and practice its fundamentals. This chapter also considers what program leaders can do to facilitate teachers' skills for working with families.

We then turn in Chapter 7 to the issue of productively managing the inevitable disequilibrium and conflicts that arise in anti-bias work as part of the dynamics of change. In Chapter 8 we address strategies for documenting and assessing progress in a program and staff's anti-bias transformation. In Chapter 9 we examine the contentious issue of required standards and assessment tools as these may support or hinder anti-bias work. We also relate strategies that leaders in diversity and equity work draw on to meet the challenges of standards. Then, in Chapter 10, we conclude with our personal reflections on sustaining an anti-bias vision and journey.

Many of the stories and examples in this book are based on Debbie's and John's experiences over the course of their long careers as teachers and directors in various settings. Details have been changed or made into composites to protect anonymity and to help illustrate particular concepts and ideas. In particular, we have drawn from Debbie's experience as director of the Eliot–Pearson Children's School (EPCS) at Tufts University from 1996 to 2013 and from John's experience as executive director of the Child Study and Development Center (CSDC) at the University of New Hampshire from 2003 to 2013. In addition, we have included comments collected from teachers and parents at EPCS and teachers from CSDC throughout the chapters to bring their voices into our exploration of anti-bias change.

We recognize that the terms people use in diversity and equity work vary, depending on their analysis of issues and strategies for addressing the issues. In addition, the same term may have different meanings, again depending on people's viewpoint about diversity and equity. In Figure I.1 we provide our definitions of the main terms found throughout the chapters.

Figure I.1. Definitions of Terms

Anti-Bias education (ABE). An approach that includes addressing issues of personal and social identity, social–emotional relationships with people different from oneself, prejudice, discrimination, critical thinking, and taking action for fairness with children. It also includes an emphasis on adult anti-bias growth and understanding of the systemic dynamics of oppression. Throughout this book we have included *culturally relevant care and education* (defined below) within this concept.

Culturally relevant care and education. A framework and approach in which the program's pedagogy, curriculum, and environment are responsive and relevant to differences in the culture of all individuals and groups. Historically, schools have only reflected the dominant culture (see below) and have expected other groups to assimilate.

Diversity. We use this term in its broadest sense—inclusive of all people's racial identity, ethnicity, family culture, gender, class, sexual orientation, and ability. Diversity exists in the differences *among* people and groups. It is not a term that refers to some people and not to others. The term *anti-bias* includes the concept of diversity. Strategically, it is sometimes useful to use the term "diversity" instead of "anti-bias" because it is more accessible or acceptable in a specific situation.

Diversity/equity education. An inclusive term for a range of educational approaches, all of which address various facets of diversity, inclusion, and fairness. Anti-bias education is one such approach. Diversity and equity also signify that the power relationships and dynamics between people of different backgrounds are equal. This means that everyone gets an equivalent place at the table and opportunities to use their voice.

Dominant (mainstream, majority, agent) culture. The term used to refer to the rules, values, language, and worldview of the groups with economic and political power in a society. In the United States, the dominant group has historically been White, Christian, affluent, heterosexual, able-bodied, and male. This dominant group defines its way of life as the "normal" and right way to live, and judges others who differ from this standard.

Early childhood care and education (ECCE). Often used interchangeably with early childhood education (ECE), we believe ECCE is a more inclusive term because it includes child care as well as preschools and other education and care institutions serving young children. The acronym is used throughout the book.

Family. We primarily use this term instead of "parents and/or guardians." It is a more inclusive way to describe the realities of the diversity of children's primary caregivers and is the increasingly preferred term among many ECCE professionals.

Leader/leadership. In this book we specifically focus on the role of *positional* leaders in ECCE programs, that is, those responsible for the supervision and development of staff, policy development, and broad oversight of the program mission and vision. We also recognize the importance of supporting and developing the *leadership* capacity of staff and family members when seeking to create deep and enduring change in values, structures, and practice.

Figure I.1. Definitions of Terms, Continued

Program(s). An inclusive term for the range of group care and education programs serving young children, including preschools, schools, after-school programs, and child-care centers. While the approach and strategies described in this book can be adapted for use in family child care and other home-based settings, they are most relevant to institutions with a number of staff and serving larger groups of children and families.

Program leader. We use this term to be inclusive of a wide range of specific terms for this professional role (as noted above under the term *Leader*), including director, center manager, and principal. This diversity of terminology reflects the diverse organizational forms that early childhood care and education takes. In some programs this executive role may be shared by more than one person.

Staff. All the employees in the program—teachers as well as the business manager, administrative assistant, cook, nurse, and so on. We use teachers to refer to staff members who have some form of classroom teaching responsibility, including assistant teachers, aides, and interns. Educators is used as a broader term that includes teachers and other personnel with educational responsibilities such as educational coordinators, assistant directors, and special education leaders.

MEET THE AUTHORS

This book comes out of our personal and professional journeys pursuing the vision of anti-bias education. As leaders of early childhood centers, Debbie and John were engaged in the work of initiating, growing, and sustaining anti-bias education programs for many years. Louise has been writing and speaking about anti-bias education with early childhood teachers throughout the United States and internationally since 1989. The following minibiographies describe the life and work influences that shaped who we are and informed our professional choices including the writing of this book.

Debbie's Story

My professional journey as an anti-bias educator has roots in my personal story. I am a third-generation Chinese American born in New York City, but have lived and taught in diverse communities throughout the United States as well as overseas. My parents were the first generation in their families to go to college and fulfill the American dream. My grandparents were the typical Chinese immigrants, opening a Chinese restaurant and a Chinese laundry. As a person of color growing up in predominately White communities during the 1950s and 1960s, I experienced discrimination and prejudice, but also the power of activism through the civil rights movement. I met my husband, an Irish American, in college; we have two adult children and a multiracial granddaughter. Finding communities to raise our children that were accepting of differences was important to us.

My personal experiences grounded my professional career in diversity work. My passion to work in diverse communities led me from Bolivia to Taiwan, Hong Kong and New Mexico and to the inner cities of Philadelphia, New York, and Boston. Diversity and anti-bias work was the framework I lived and brought to the classroom, whether my students were children, families, teenagers, or college students. As a teacher and leader, I was determined to create a community that would be safe and supportive of all kinds of differences.

In one of my first jobs as a preschool teacher, I remember a parent coming to me and saying, "I don't want my child to play with those black dolls in the dramatic play corner. She may grow up and marry a Black person." I remember feeling very angry with this parent. In my mind and heart I called him a racist; my job was to save the child. I was very indignant and radical about it. Forty years later, when I hear the same comments, I have a very different approach. I ask myself, "Where is this person coming from; why do they feel that way?" I try to *dialogue*. My goal is to learn from each person, to listen, be nonjudgmental. Nothing is all black and white; life is gray.

As director of the Eliot–Pearson Children's School (EPCS) for 17 years, I had the opportunity to think strategically about shifting the whole program to an anti-bias perspective. A director has the opportunity to systematically plan change from admissions and hiring, to working with teachers and families, to classrooms and children. As a leader and a Person of Color, I did not want my staff to want to "do" anti-bias work because it was important to me, but because it was the right thing to do. The leader provides the vision and direction, but wants the motivation for change to bubble up, not just trickle down. I believe in a collaborative style of leadership and consensus building.

When I first came to the school, it was known for its inclusion model of integrating children with special needs with typically developing children. One of the first strategic shifts I did was expand the definition of inclusion to include all kinds of differences. Ability differences became just another kind of difference at the school.

I have learned that conflict is inevitable; it is not to be avoided or feared. While my Chinese culture emphasized not rocking the boat, and keeping peace and harmony, my professional experience taught me "conflict and tension" is when growth happens. It is an indicator of change. We may have different viewpoints, but when we struggle together, and really listen, we are often surprised. Do not make assumptions. Agree to disagree. Acknowledge our own mistakes. Be humble. Now I want to guide leaders to create communities that not only support differences but also support a climate that allows discomfort around conflict and risk taking. This is my work, professionally and personally, of living in a diverse world.

John's Story

As an Anglo-Australian, my beginnings were marked by middle- and upper-class (unearned) privileges and hearing stories of family trees proudly rooted in the nobility of Scotland and Germany. As the son of a small-town doctor, I recall the status afforded to my family and the entitlement of attending a private boarding school for boys in the city. My social class provided opportunities to travel and interact in cultures very different from my own (e.g., in Indonesia and Papua New Guinea). I vividly remember the silence I received from those around me when I, as a young child, made naive observations about difference. It was during my adolescence and teacher training that I began to question injustices on many levels; I marched in the student union, protested education cuts, and rallied for gay rights.

As a male in the early childhood field (one of only a few at that time in Australia), I became focused more passionately on issues of sexism and homophobia in my profession and the broader society. During the 1970s I sought out children's books featuring women in nonstereotypical professional roles and supported boys to feel at home in the dress-up area. My decade as a preschool teacher and director in Australia included contact with families from differing backgrounds. Looking back, my assumptions, experience, and knowledge base meant that these differences often remained invisible in my classroom and consciousness. I recall now with disbelief that I dressed up each year as Santa Claus for Christmas celebrations at my Australian preschool—oblivious to the message of exclusion for some families.

While at home with liberal views, my sojourn to Pacific Oaks College in California for graduate work brought me into contact with the U.S. cultural milieu. The strong women mentors there (including Louise Derman-Sparks) challenged me to examine my identity, and introduced me to the work of Paulo Freire. This was a qualitative shift from liberal convenience, through disequilibrium, to a deeper understanding of oppression, bias, and social justice.

Later, I had the good fortune to work as Debbie LeeKeenan's graduate assistant at the University of Massachusetts lab school while completing my doctorate. My diversity education continued as a faculty member at the Pacific Oaks campus in Seattle for a decade, where I had the powerful experience of being the only White male on a collaborative and multicultural staff. During this time, I was a member of the Culturally Relevant Anti-Bias Education Leadership group and performed in the Seattle Theater of Liberation troupe. Most significantly, I embarked with my partner on the complex journey of raising two children with social justice values.

From 2003 to 2013, I made the leap between theory and practice as the executive director at the Child Study and Development Center (CSDC) at the University of New Hampshire. When considering the possibility of moving there, I was asked on occasion, "Why would you want to pursue anti-bias education in rural New Hampshire where everyone is the same?" I remember Louise advising me: "If not you, who?" While explicit about my intentions, I soon realized that I would face many challenges in a setting where diversity was often hidden or nonexistent. This situation drove home the importance of identifying allies—of which there were many among the incredible staff and families at the center—that could help me in initiating change. It was during this time that I rediscovered my collaborative relationship with Debbie, who was continuing her anti-bias journey as director of Eliot–Pearson Children's School.

Louise's Story

I have been an educator and activist for social justice for much of my 74 years. I grew up in a White, Jewish American, working-class family in Brooklyn and Manhattan, New York. I learned about activism from an early age, by observing and listening and by accompanying my parents on some of their community activism work. I went to public schools, from kindergarten through college. In elementary and junior high school, a few very good teachers illuminated the possibilities of caring and meaningful education. Fortunate to attend a high school more diverse than most in New York City at that time and with the civil rights and anti-nuclear-bomb movements blossoming, I began becoming an activist in my own right.

Over the many years of doing social justice and anti-bias work, I have had to come to a critical understanding of the multiple parts of my identity—especially my racial, class, and gender identities. While the antiracism movement challenged me to critically examine my role on the *advantaged* side of societal power, the women's movement challenged me, as a woman, to comprehend the *disadvantaged* side of societal power. On the other hand, being heterosexual gave me societal legitimacy and important legal rights. In my family of origin, I was working class. As a college professor—a different socioeconomic status—I continue to identify with my working-class and activist roots.

I come to this book with a perspective honed by my scores of years working in early childhood education. I began as a teacher of 3- and 4-year-olds in the Perry Preschool Project in Ypsilanti, Michigan. My one experience as an early childhood program director was brief, when I led a small cooperative child-care center for 3 years. It was there that I first began exploring children's thinking about diversity and fairness—seeds that ultimately grew into the anti-bias curriculum approach. Then, my many years as a faculty member of Pacific Oaks College enabled me to study, collaborate, teach, and write about the interwoven issues of identity and attitude development and change in both children and adults. Since the 1989 publication of *Anti-Bias Curriculum: Tools for Empowering Young Children*, which I developed with the Anti-Bias Curriculum Task Force at Pacific Oaks College and Children's School, I have had the very informative and exhilarating opportunity to talk with thousands of early childhood educators and observe outstanding anti-bias education in the United States and several other countries. These learning encounters convinced me of the pivotal role of the program leader in growing anti-bias education in their particular settings.

Realizing that there was little information available about how to do this, I knew that a new book was in order. Since I believe strongly in basing what I write about anti-bias education on knowledge grounded in people's work and life experiences, I needed to connect with individuals actually leading effective early childhood anti-bias education programs. So, Debbie and John entered the picture. I had observed their programs, which served quite different populations, and was excited about what was happening with the children, as well as how they had strategically introduced and grown anti-bias work with the staff and families.

* * *

Now, together we embark on the lessons we have learned about the journey of building an anti-bias ECCE program. We hope that you join us—and through your own endeavors, add further knowledge and insights about the leader's role in this essential work.

CHAPTER 1

Pursuing the Anti-Bias Vision
The Conceptual Framework

Early childhood centers can . . . become places that respond to the longings for community, meaningful relationships, a sense of belonging, and an exuberant experience of learning about the world. . . . [They] can give the children and adults involved an experience of empowerment, of democracy in action, so that they will have the will and know-how to make this a priority in our country.

—Carter & Curtis (2010, p. 13)

Hundreds of thousands of children from many diverse backgrounds live a significant part of their childhoods in early childhood programs (Carter & Curtis, 2010). The diversity among children attending early childhood programs continues to increase, as a reflection of the nation's changing demographic realities (U.S. Census Bureau, 2012). The children's diverse ethnicities, cultures, religions, languages, and family structures bring both vibrancy and complexities to our communities. Ensuring that all early childhood care and education programs are places where all children and families are visible and thrive requires educators to pursue a "relentless commitment to equity, voice, and social justice" (Kugelmass, 2004, p. 14). Anti-bias education, or ABE (see our definition in Figure I.1 in the Introduction), can play a significant role in this pursuit. Program leaders are central to building the anti-bias education programs that can make this commitment to social justice a reality for all young children and their families.

In this first chapter we discuss the central ideas underlying the philosophy of anti-bias education. This includes: (1) a review of anti-bias education, (2) what it takes organizationally to become an anti-bias program, (3) what adults need to know in order to pursue an ABE approach, (4) the phases of antiracism identity development, and (5) an exploration of "contested-ground" issues in ECCE.

REVIEWING ANTI-BIAS EDUCATION

The heart of anti-bias education is a vision of a world in which all children and families can become successful, contributing members of their society. To achieve this goal, they need to experience affirmation of their identities and cultural ways of being, and learn how to live and work together in diverse and inclusive environments (Derman-Sparks & Edwards, 2010). The anti-bias vision incorporates the basic human rights described in the United Nations Convention on the Rights of the Child (UNICEF, 1990), which embrace the right to an identity, to be free from discrimination, to express opinions, and to participate actively in the community.

Anti-bias education supports children in developing a fuller, truer understanding of themselves and the world, and strengthens their sense of themselves as capable, empowered people. They have a better chance to develop curiosity, openness to multiple perspectives, and critical-thinking skills. They can also develop their ability to resist the harm that prejudice, misinformation, and discrimination do to their sense of competence and efficacy. These social–emotional and cognitive abilities increase the likelihood that children of all backgrounds will be able to navigate the larger worlds of school and community more constructively and effectively. As Jack P. Shonkoff, M.D., Chair of the National Scientific Council on the Developing Child, makes clear:

> There is a very strong science of emotional development and social development. . . . We have a great deal of brain research that tells us how emotions are very much embedded in the architecture of the brain and the function of the brain. . . . Our conclusion from the science is that absolutely early literacy experiences are very important for young children, but they're no more important than paying attention to children's social health and their emotional well-being. (Boulton, n.d.)

Four core goals of anti-bias education form a framework for guiding practice in a program's learning environment, curriculum, and child-teacher interactions. These goals take into account the body of research about how children construct their identity and attitudes and about the impact of racism and other "isms" on these developmental processes. Such research about children has been accumulating for more than 50 years (e.g., Beonson & Merryman, 2009; Clark, 1963; Clark & Clark, 1947; Goodman, 1952; Hirschfeld, 2008; P. A. Katz, 1976; Lane, 2008; Mac Naughton & Davis, 2009; Ramsey, 2004; Tatum, 1997; Trager & Radke Yarrow, 1952; Van Ausdale & Feagin, 2001). As late as 2010, a CNN commissioned study about children's racial attitudes, under the direction of Dr. Margaret Beale Spencer, supported previous research findings that White and Black children held a preference toward lighter skin color ("Study: White and Black Children Biased Toward Lighter Skin," 2010).

The anti-bias education goals are for children of all family backgrounds and communities, and each goal interacts with and builds on the others. The four goals are the following:

Goal 1: Each child will demonstrate self-awareness, confidence, family pride, and positive social identities.

Goal 2: Each child will express comfort and joy with human diversity; accurate language for human differences; and deep, caring human connections.

Goal 3: Each child will increasingly recognize unfairness, have language to describe unfairness, and understand that unfairness hurts.

Goal 4: Each child will demonstrate empowerment and the skills to act, with others or alone, against prejudice and/or discriminatory actions. (Derman-Sparks & Edwards, 2010, p. xiv)

BECOMING AN ANTI-BIAS PROGRAM

An anti-bias program puts diversity and equity goals at the center of all aspects of its organization and daily life. It involves much more than adding new materials and activities into the already existing learning environment. Rather, broad systemic changes are necessary. The learning environment and curriculum, as well as program policies, structures, procedures, and processes, all come into play. Change also includes the perspectives and attitudes of the individuals who serve the children and families. In sum, it is "a process, not an event" (Kugelmass, 2004, p. 6).

Significant organizational change requires shared commitments, a collaborative process, and facilitation (Kugelmass, 2004). It also calls for developmental growth in the program leader and staff. While the urgency to implement anti-bias education is great from the perspective of the children's needs, the process of change happens over time; an anti-bias education leader must plan for the long haul. Successful anti-bias education change needs an intentional and thoughtful strategic approach.

Two central dynamics of organizational change come into play. One is shifting the cultural core of the program; the second is recognizing the impact of the process of change on the stakeholders. As the program leader, you have a primary role in facilitating both dynamics.

Shifting the Culture of the ECCE Program

While the importance of culturally relevant ECCE programs is a major theme in the field, too many early childhood programs continue to ground their environment, curriculum, teaching styles, and language in the dominant culture (as defined in Figure I.1 in the Introduction). Staff may act out societal power relationships of advantage and disadvantage and socially prevalent biases, even if they are not aware of what is happening.

The dynamics of dominant-culture–centered early childhood programs push other viewpoints to the margins—even when the majority of families at the program come from other cultural backgrounds. This means that a large number of young children experience two differing cultural contexts every day.

Worse, children may experience their home culture as invisible or inferior. When teachers use child development norms and criteria based on dominant group culture to judge the ability of children from other cultural groups, the teachers are hindered in seeing the actual developmental abilities and growth of many children. This dynamic automatically advantages children from the dominant culture group and disadvantages children from nondominant groups.

The more discontinuity young children face, the more likely they are to find that what they are learning in their family about how to be in the world, including their home language, does not work for them outside their family. The lack of familiarity with a program's practices makes it harder for them to adjust, to build strong relationships, to act and feel competent, and to feel secure. Conversely, the more continuity between home and school a child experiences, the better able they are to be active, competent participants, and to feel respected for who they are.

Minimizing cultural discontinuity between home and school programs and eliminating indicators of discounting or prejudice against a child's home culture foster an equal playing field for all the children. Young children thrive when their early childhood program integrates their home languages and cultures into all of its operations. Developmentally appropriate programs pay attention to the social and cultural contexts in which each child lives, and not just to a child's individual characteristics (National Association for the Education of Young Children [NAEYC], 1995).

Building an anti-bias ECCE program requires shifting the dominant-culture core of a program's thinking, organizational structures, and practice. It means intentionally moving to a many-cultures, anti-bias approach. Shifting the culture of a program brings groups at the margin of ECCE theory and practice into the center of all that happens. Shifting the culture also requires adjustment to the dominant and traditional approaches to ECCE to incorporate other ways of thinking and doing (Anderson & Collins, 1997).

Shifting the culture of a program calls for a broad vision of equity and inclusion and an intentional effort to create change. It demands attention to the seemingly small and everyday details of a program's life, as well as to the broader structures, relationships, and teaching practices. An anti-bias program continually evolves as the composition and structure of the program changes. Doing all of this requires strong leadership and engagement from the various stakeholders in the program or organization.

Recognizing the Response to Change

Change inevitably brings disequilibrium, dissonance, and conflicts—until specific changes become part of everyday life. There will likely be differences about what to change and how to carry out agreed-upon changes, or even whether to change at all.

Some program stakeholders (e.g., staff, families, administration) may fear that creating a program where the dominant culture shares space with other perspectives is a threat to their own rights, even though the goal is for *everyone* to have a voice and place. Similarly, some may fear that a shift away from the dominant culture approach requires abandoning all they have previously learned about creating quality early childhood programs. Staff or family members who fear loss of their own way of life or of program quality may try to resist change. The discomforts of disequilibrium push people to search for solutions that will bring equilibrium again—either retreating to the safety of familiar ways or, hopefully, searching for fresh perspectives. Finding ways to move the organization and its individual members closer to anti-bias education goals is a crucial part of the anti-bias education leadership role.

Even when everyone wants change, people will still experience disequilibrium. Inevitably, disagreements will arise about which aspects of the policy, structures, and curriculum to work on and with what strategies. The organization's stakeholders may want different timetables. Some may want to shift the culture of the program faster than the rest of the staff are willing to take on. Some may want it to take longer or have a different sequence.

Even in the midst of change, the pull to keep things as they are (the status quo) will arise. We like to compare this dynamic to the function of the "default" mode on a computer. If the font of a computer is changed from its default mode to another font, the computer reverts to the default the next time it is used. Making change rarely follows a clean, linear course of action. A program may make progress in one arena, but hit resistance to change in another arena. From time to time, everyone needs a brief respite before taking up the challenge once again. External events may open up and support changes on a specific aspect of diversity, or they may create bumps in the road.

CHANGING ADULT CONSCIOUSNESS AND BEHAVIOR

Realistically, ECCE practitioners who have been absorbing their families' and societal assumptions, stereotypes, and prejudices about human identity since childhood cannot be expected to suddenly teach children not to absorb these same beliefs and attitudes. And yet that is exactly what a program leader may expect.

The learning goals for adults reflect current thinking about identity as a combination of social group membership and individual life experiences. Exploring and deepening an individual's understanding of one's own and others' social identities and their influence on perspectives and behaviors are important components of becoming effective anti-bias educators.

Social Identity

William Cross's (1991) pioneering analysis of the studies of African American identity development compellingly argued for a societal component to self-concept. Calling it "reference group orientation," in contrast to "personal identity," Cross used these two categories to re-conceptualize thinking about the impact of racism on African Americans' identity. His work remains central to anti-bias education. In this book, we use the term *social identity* instead of *reference group orientation*.

Everyone has many social identities in addition to an individual personal identity. Social identities connect individuals to larger groups beyond their family. They comprise characteristics such as people's racial and ethnic identity, gender, culture, religion, language, economic class, family structure, sexual orientation, and abilities, as these characteristics are defined by the society in which people live. Social identities play a significant role in how an individual is seen and treated by others, and they affect access to the society's institutions, such as education, health, and the legal system (Derman-Sparks & Edwards, 2010).

How an individual feels personally about various social identities may stand in opposition to the societal realities of advantage and disadvantage connected to them. For example, social discrimination and negative messages about being "working class" do not necessarily stop people from being personally proud of their family background.

The definitions and ideas regarding various social identities are not a static situation. Because of movements for social justice, as well as specific social–political–economic dynamics, the definition, criteria, and the specific advantages or disadvantages connected to social identities have legally changed throughout U.S. history. One example is the changes in women's right to property, education, the vote, jobs, and reproductive choice. Another is the changing status and right of people who are gay, lesbian, transgender, or bisexual to marry and receive partner benefits. This expanded equality and human rights transform how individuals think about themselves and how others view them.

Adult Learning Goals

Five anti-bias learning goals for adults complement the goals for children. These are as follows:

1. Increase your awareness and understanding of your own social identity in its many facets (gender, race, ethnicity, economic class, family structure, religion, sexual orientation, abilities/disabilities) and your own cultural contexts, both childhood and current.
2. Examine what you have learned about differences, connection, and what you enjoy or fear across lines of human diversity.

3. Identify how you have been advantaged or disadvantaged by the "isms" (racism, sexism, classism, ablism, heterosexism) and the stereotypes or prejudices you have absorbed about yourself or others.
4. Explore your ideas, feelings, and experiences of social justice activism.
5. Open up dialogue with colleagues and families about all these goals. (Derman-Sparks & Edwards, 2010, p. 21)

Too few ECCE teacher preparation programs adequately engage students in serious learning about culturally responsive and anti-bias education or in the self-reflection and growth that this approach requires (Ray, Bowman, & Robbins, 2006). Similarly, many already practicing teachers have not had sufficient training. They may have gone to a conference presentation or workshop in their school or center, but these quick-fix approaches do not provide more than surface learning (Dunst & Trivette, 2012).

Program leaders need to shoulder a large part of the task of facilitating their staff's growth toward achieving the adult anti-bias goals. To do so, they must also accept the adult ABE goals as valid and make them their own. This means working on the five adult goals oneself before facilitating staff anti-bias development, as well as continuing to work on them along with staff.

UNDERSTANDING THE PHASES OF ADULT ANTI-BIAS DEVELOPMENT

Several antiracism educators and psychologists (Cross, 1991; Derman-Sparks & Phillips, 1997; Helms, 1993, 1995; Tatum, 1992, 1994; Wijeyesinghe & Jackson, 2012) write about the developmental patterns or phases in the adult racial-identity journey among Whites and among People of Color. These offer a useful perspective for understanding the changes that staff experience as they go on their journey of developing anti-bias education understanding and skills. You may recognize some of the characteristics of these phases as similar to what you have and are experiencing on your own anti-bias journey. In this section, we convert the antiracism stages to the consciousness and behaviors we have documented among staff (and ourselves) over many years as ECCE leaders.

Staff in any given ECCE program will likely be at different phases in their awareness, interest, and knowledge of the anti-bias approach. Some will express enthusiasm, readiness, and engagement. They may show some of the characteristics of the second or third phases of the anti-bias developmental path. Others will need encouragement to begin, showing the characteristics of people in the beginning phases of the anti-bias journey.

Each individual's growth also may look different in relation to the various areas of social identity. This includes people's attitudes and behavior, as well as their understanding of the advantages or disadvantages that society connects to the various kinds of identities (Nieto, 2010). For example, an individual may be farther on the anti-bias journey in regard to gender and sexism, than in comprehension of racism. Each person's particular "social identity portrait" carries different areas of societal advantage and disadvantage, which also influences the anti-bias journey.

We urge you to refer to this discussion of the phases of the anti-bias journey as you create an initial portrait of your program (see Chapter 3), work with your staff (Chapters 4 and 6), and document their growth (Chapter 8). It can be a helpful framework for scaffolding your anti-bias work with individual staff members and with the program as a whole. It suggests when to challenge people to move ahead on their anti-bias journey, and when not to push people too fast, so that they stop expressing their ideas and feelings and growth stops. Understanding the journey of staff also enables the program leader to appreciate both the common dynamics and the individual differences in the anti-bias journey.

Before the Journey Begins

Denial of the significance of diversity and bias indicates that a staff member is not yet on the anti-bias education journey. It is expressed in comments such as "I have no prejudices so don't need to do this"; "Children do not care about differences among people"; "I do not see any awareness or interest from them."

Teachers in programs primarily serving White children, often use the rationale that "it isn't that we are not interested in diversity, but we are not a diverse school" to deny the need for anti-bias education. They usually refer to a lack of racial or ethnic diversity, ignoring the fact that children absorb misinformation and biases whether or not they have direct contact with people different from themselves. Moreover, diversity comes in multiple forms (e.g., economic class, ethnic/cultural groups, religion, gender roles, abilities), so all groups of children (even when all come from the same ethnic background) represent some diversity.

Denial of the need for anti-bias education may also come from teachers in programs only serving children of color. Their reasons tend to take the form of "we have to focus on fostering our children's positive identity; we do not have time to concern ourselves with other groups." In *Anti-Bias Education for Young Children and Ourselves* (Derman-Sparks & Edwards, 2010), Carol Brunson Day offers her insights about this issue:

People of Color often have the feeling that anti-bias education is work that Whites need to do, because the sources of racism come from White history and culture. They question its relevancy for children of color, for whom they believe empowerment is the key issue. White children definitely need anti-bias education. So, too, do children of color, although the specific work differs from that with White children. Educational efforts that prevent internalized oppression by fostering strong personal and social identities and counter prejudices about *other* groups of color are two essential tasks that are part of the larger anti-bias work. We also need to create alliances to achieve our shared ultimate goal of a more equitable society. (p. 7)

Resistance from members of the dominant social identity groups may also come from their anxiety that anti-bias education will leave them out (a reversal of the current dominant-culture–centered approach where many groups are invisible in the curriculum and learning environment). Comments include "My family is White and I don't see myself in the center as much as I did before. There are photos of diverse families, but I'm not there," or "I do not want my children to be prejudiced, but where do White people fit in an anti-bias curriculum?" While an anti-bias approach includes everyone—including White people—it is true that dominant-culture groups have to share space and attention with others. When an ECCE program shifts toward an anti-bias culture, it can feel to some members of the dominant culture like these changes have taken their world away from them.

When you have staff in the prejourney phase, the challenge is to identify what aspects of diversity and bias connect with their lives and to tap into their feelings. It is important to ascertain if those staff members are really separating themselves from issues of diversity and bias or are just being silent about their thoughts and feelings. A second key is to help staff in this phase discover the realities of diversity and bias in children's lives.

Beginning to Face the Issues

People embarking on their first steps on the anti-bias journey begin to look critically at their identity and attitudes. Signs include openness, honesty, and taking risks in storytelling about who they are. As staff members are more open about their experiences and feelings about diversity, they also discover how much anti-bias issues are a part of their lives. You also discover how much complexity exists in their lives.

Another indicator of this phase is an individual's realization that everyone has a culture and openness to exploring its characteristics. This is often more difficult for White people since their European ancestors, as immigrants, "melted" (assimilated) their heritage to form the new society of the United States. Some White people feel a sense of loss, wondering where they go to learn about their families' original cultural identities. They may even express envy of nondominant cultural groups who know their cultural identity.

A third indicator is a teacher's "seeing" that children are noticing and have ideas about differences, and taking some initial steps in the classroom to address these through conversations with the children and making environmental changes. At this point teachers may become open to sharing uncertainties about how to respond to children's questions and negative comments about various aspects of diversity and express interest in enhancing their skills.

Another indicator of movement in anti-bias development is openness to learning about the various ways families raise their children and seeing the need to learn *from* families. Teachers also show willingness to interact with families about childrearing, even if they feel uncomfortable because they are not sure of what to say or worry that their questions will offend a family.

As individuals begin to uncover their own issues and understand how bias harms children's development, they may show signs of emotional and intellectual disequilibrium. People express pain, guilt, anger, or try to divert the conversation to a more familiar and comfortable topic. In some cases, an individual may respond to disequilibrium by wanting to go back to denial: "I'm all for diversity, but aren't we talking too much about it?"

Committing to the Anti-Bias Education Journey and Work

By this phase, staff members demonstrate continuing reflection about themselves and their work, and engagement with ongoing learning. As a college student in a class about racism and human development declared, "It feels like I had this big closet to clean out . . . and was now trying to decide what stayed, what needed fixing, and what to throw out. It's a big job, but it feels great" (Derman-Sparks & Phillips, 1997, p. 112).

In this phase, it is important to ensure that staff members do not view anti-bias ideas as only applicable to children, but also engage in critical self-reflection. One marker is evidence of growth in staff members' understanding of their social identities and appreciating the relationship between identity and their actions as a teacher. For example, a teacher may indicate that she realizes that knowing who she is strengthens the work she does with the children and families on a daily basis. Families whose backgrounds are similar to or different from hers will benefit by her greater self-insight.

Ownership of anti-bias education work is another key indicator. This includes staff implementing anti-bias education because it is what they want to do, rather than something they are doing to please the program leader. Evidence of ownership includes teachers regularly sharing anecdotes about children's interest in diversity and signs of discomfort or early prejudice, and wanting to problem-solve ways to address what they are observing. They actively raise conversations about differences in the classroom with children and initiate activities. Although they may still not be comfortable with the fourth anti-bias goal of taking action against injustice, teachers do begin to take the initiative in moving the anti-bias mission forward.

Anti-Bias Education as the Norm

Not only do staff members routinely integrate anti-bias values and concepts into the various experiences in their daily curriculum, they also set goals for themselves that reflect their commitment to ongoing anti-bias education. For example, one teacher affirms that she plans to build her understanding of how to include same-sex families in her planned unit about families; another commits to focus on improving her "teachable moment" skills in responding to children's questions and comments; a third decides to take a class in Spanish, given the increasing number of Spanish-speaking families in her school.

At this phase in the journey, engaging in anti-bias education becomes a partnership among teachers and the program leader. One key indicator is that staff hold their leader accountable to the program's anti-bias education mission. John describes such a moment at his center:

> We had a conversation about whether to wear flip-flops or not at work, which led to a serious conversation around the cost of footwear. Some staff said, "I know you have expensive comfy leather sandals, but I can't afford them." I just had to laugh and say, "Well I suppose I asked for that!"

Another marker of this phase is comfort working with families on anti-bias issues. For example, when teachers invite family members to come in and share something from their family culture, they sometimes encounter confusion about what "culture" means. Teachers now have the language they need to explain that *everyone* has a culture. The fact that the teachers are able to understand family culture in relation to themselves, allows them to do this work in a more complex way with parents.

As you use these phases to help identify next steps in staff's anti-bias work, keep in mind that individual journeys always have their own specific variations. Individuals may also be in different phases of development on various anti-bias issues.

RECOGNIZING CONTESTED GROUNDS FOR ANTI-BIAS EDUCATION

We use the concept of "contested grounds" to signify figurative spaces where diverging, contending views of what does and should count as core values, knowledge, policies, and actions open up possibilities for changes in thinking and practice. The generally accepted principles and practices of ECCE generate several pivotal contested grounds for anti-bias education thinking and practice including the role of ECCE, the sources of developmental theory, and the nature of children's identity development. These issues reflect core contradictions in our society's ideology, policies, and actions regarding diversity and equality. Anti-bias education leaders must understand these contested-ground issues well because they do influence the dynamics of leadership.

The Role of ECCE

Clarifying your own beliefs about the role of early childhood care and education in the larger society is one aspect of building an anti-bias program. We view these values as a powerful bridge between the child's family and society. How this bridge gets constructed matters, profoundly affecting how young children experience their ECCE program. For example, is it a one-way bridge for primarily moving children into the dominant society, or a two-way bridge that enables children to become bicultural? Our diverse society is complex with strong, contradictory themes and practices regarding how we treat human beings. The history of ECCE programs reflects these contradictions. Values of equality and supporting all children and families, regardless of their heritage and status in society, are strong themes in that history, as is the goal of preparing children to be ready for society as it is, with its existing social and economic inequities.

These often-conflicting themes appear in the current debate about whether the role of ECCE programs is to enable children to thrive in their home culture and also successfully navigate in mainstream schools or to push for children's assimilation into the dominant society by losing much of their home culture. The current debates and conflicting policies and practices about English-only early childhood education versus dual-language and bilingual education pose one example of the larger competing perspectives on the purpose of early childhood education as a bridge between family and society. These differing viewpoints also generate conflicting beliefs about the criteria for quality education and the need for and type of diversity and equity education.

The historical significance afforded family and community life in the ECCE field, as well as a strong thread of belief in the value of all children and families, creates a unique opportunity for building programs that foster a many-cultures and equitable understanding of child development and early childhood education practice.

Development Theories and Practices

Historically both child development theories and the developmentally appropriate practices based on these theories have reflected the socialization norms and practices of the dominant group in the United States (Mallory & New, 1994). This thinking has traditionally pushed other cultural viewpoints to the margins, even in very diverse settings. On the other hand, challenges to the dominant-culture-only approach to children's development and criteria for quality programs are becoming a part of the current ECCE discourse and principles. Advocating for culturally appropriate care appears in the latest revision of NAEYC's developmentally appropriate practices book (Copple & Bredekamp, 2009), and in their position paper on cultural and linguistic diversity (NAEYC, 1995). The well-respected "Program for Infant/Toddler Care," WestEd's newest edition of their *A Guide to Culturally Sensitive Care* (Virmani & Mangione, 2013) also offers up-to-date thinking about the role of culture and bias in young children's development.

These additions to the knowledge base of ECCE are significant and positive, but much more requires doing. Reyna Hernandez (2011), Research and Policy Associate at the Latino Policy Forum, explains:

At the national and state level, early childhood leaders committed to providing high-quality services struggle with integrating the concepts of linguistic and cultural diversity into the broader definition of high quality. . . . [Yet] diversity issues are relevant in all early childhood settings, whether school-, center-, or home-based, and whether publicly or privately funded. (p. 1)

We argue that Hernandez's point extends to the diversity and inequity issues in ECCE connected to gender, class, ability, and family diversity.

Building an ECCE program that integrates a many-cultures perspective obliges leaders and staff to accept that customary ways of working are not always the only ways. As Carol Brunson Day explains:

We can learn principles for creating culturally consistent programs. However, there is no recipe for being there. The *there* is built by you with families and staff. It is always a dynamic process and depends on the people who are together in a program at any given time. . . . If you stay open to the fact that your way is not the only right way, trust in the ability of people to figure out differences, and really work on it, you can get to where you want your classroom to be. When everyone has access to deciding on a solution that works for him or her, then there is real equality. (Quoted in Derman-Sparks & Edwards, 2010, p. 61)

Children's Identity Development

The questions of whether societal prejudices affect young children's development and how ECCE should address this influence also create contested ground. Traditionally in ECCE, the subject of young children and prejudice was largely invisible, although pioneering research about this subject began as early as 1926 and major work appeared in the 1950s. In fact, Clark's (1963) pioneering research played a key role in the U.S. Supreme Court's historic 1954 school desegregation decision (Clark, 1988). Active discussion and debate about children and racism reemerged in the 1970s and 1980s, influenced by the civil rights movement. By the 1990s, addressing the impact of the larger society on young children's construction of identity and attitudes became a part of ECCE discourse.

Advocates argue that it is both necessary and developmentally appropriate to integrate issues of diversity and equity that relate to young children's lives into the curriculum. Research about the impact of racism (and other forms of prejudice and discrimination) on children informs anti-bias education. Many ECCE professionals now subscribe to this thinking, and it is supported in NAEYC's *Developmentally Appropriate Practices in Early Childhood Programs Serving Children Birth Through Age 8* (Copple & Bredekamp, 2009). However, our many years of collective experience listening to early childhood professionals throughout the country indicate that many of them still believe that it is inappropriate to do so. Usually unaware of the considerable research to the contrary, some insist that young children do not notice or have ideas about human differences and prevailing societal and family prejudices. Others believe that intentionally opening up issues of diversity with young children results in their becoming prejudiced. Being very familiar with the research and analysis about children's identity and attitude development is an essential part of your anti-bias toolbox.

ANTI-BIAS EDUCATION—WITHIN REACH

ECCE programs using the anti-bias approach exist throughout the United States and internationally (e.g., B. Brown, 1998, 2008; Creaser & Dau, 1996; Mac Naughton & Davis, 2009; Murray & Urban, 2012; Van Keulen, 2004). Reflecting anti-bias education's dynamic quality, educators in various countries adapt anti-bias goals, values, and pedagogical principles to the demographic, cultural, and political characteristics of their respective contexts. These include national demographics and cultural patterns, national politics, and differences in early childhood systems and pedagogical approaches.

Anti-bias education leaders—wherever they are—must have a vision and be strategic about working toward it. They must keep their eye on the journey as well as the destination. While the urgency to do anti-bias education is great, the process of change happens over time. A slow, continuous process supports real human growth and builds skills and a committed school culture (E. Hoffman, personal communication, 2009).

In the end, anti-bias work humanizes us. Beth Wallace (1999), a former child-care center director, explains:

Anti-bias work . . . has enabled me to reclaim my vision of childcare and education as empowerment, as a vehicle for changing the world. Our work as teachers has that kind of power. Anti-bias work provides a vehicle for not just acknowledging that power, but claiming and using it to build in our classrooms and centers the kinds of communities we want to live in, models of the world we envision. (p. 155)

CHAPTER 2

Best Practices of Early Childhood Program Leaders

The Foundation for Anti-Bias Leadership

Our heritage as a field has been the continual development of early childhood leaders who have been passionate, active dreamers with our eyes on the best interest of children.

—Valora Washington (1997, p. 66)

Anti-bias leadership builds on the core principles and best leadership practices of the early childhood care and education field. These include relationships of mutual caring and respect; sharing knowledge; reflective, intentional teaching; and collaboration among staff and between staff and the program leader (G. Morgan, 2000). A belief in pushing the *"what-is to the what-might-be"* and *"seeking to impact the social good"* (Kagan & Neuman, 1997, p. 60) also historically underlies the ECCE leadership tradition. Ultimately, the leadership principles and practices for ECCE overall are also a strong foundational launching point for anti-bias education.

The leader role (as defined in Figure I.1) is central to initiating, growing, and sustaining quality ECCE programs. It is difficult for even highly trained staff to sustain their best work without supportive leaders. Leadership tasks involve thoughtfully negotiating the complexity of interactions with families, staff, children, and community members, all of which carry deep personal meaning generated by caring for other people's children (Bowman, 1997). Accordingly, effective early childhood program leaders "combine a high emphasis on results with a high emphasis on relations" (Neugebauer, 2008, p. 6).

The leader also plays a vital role in fostering anti-bias education values, relationships, and strategies as an integral part of an ECCE program's mission and daily practice. While dedicated teachers do make anti-bias education happen in their classrooms and can take on varied leadership roles, program leaders have the power to create the opportunities that enable ABE to be integrated into and sustained throughout the program (Derman-Sparks & Edwards, 2010). They can initiate organizational policy and structure changes that support ongoing anti-bias education in the classrooms and with families. Program leaders also can put into motion a strong professional development plan. Drawing on critical theory, a review of the literature, and recent research in Australia, Hard, Press and Gibson (2013) conclude that "critically informed, intentional and strategic organizational [early childhood] leadership can play a pivotal role in creating changed circumstances and opportunities for children" (p. 324).

In this chapter we review the themes in current thinking and research about ECCE leadership and consider their application to anti-bias education transformation. First, we review key aspects of program leadership, and then we look at personal traits of successful program leaders and their implications for anti-bias work. We conclude with suggestions for professional development for ECCE program leaders.

KEY ASPECTS OF ECCE PROGRAM LEADERSHIP

Those of us who work closely with children's program organizations . . . know that even a highly trained staff is unlikely to provide quality if there is an unsupportive director.

—Gwen Morgan, 2000, p. 41

In this section we consider the fundamental importance of collaborative leadership, program vision, organizational culture, a community of learners, and collaborative relationships with families to effective ECCE program leadership. As principles and practices, each of these elements interacts with and works with the other elements to build a strong, quality ECCE program. Similarly, they form the foundational core for anti-bias leadership.

Promoting Collaboration

Collaborative leadership relies on cooperation, consensus building, and shared responsibility. It assumes that teachers and other staff are thoughtful professionals whose perspective, experiences, and insights are vital to building a quality program. At its best, it is transformational and empowering. Collaborative leadership also reflects a belief in all members of a staff working as a team, rather than as a hierarchy (Bowman, 1997).

Collaborative leaders exercise power *with*, rather than power *on*, staff and families. This does not mean that program leaders give up their leadership roles, but rather that they do not over direct or simply impose their ideas without ongoing engagement of staff in discussion about program decisions. They are still responsible for setting the tone and direction, but without overdefining or overdirecting (VanderVen, 2000).

Program leaders set the direction, and provide clear expectations. They also encourage, and facilitate the development of self-awareness and reflection, confidence, and effective communication skills, provide a working knowledge of child development and learning, and offer regular support for staff's efforts to make changes. Leaders also engage staff in regular review of the program's mission and goal priorities, and ongoing individual assessment of each staff member's work (Carter & Curtis, 2010).

When teachers and other staff feel part of creating the mission, values, goals, and policies of their program, they are more likely to have a strong personal interest in helping the organization achieve results. Research indicates that "centers in which directors encouraged staff participation in decision-making exhibited significantly higher levels of staff motivation, mutual support and trust, communication, and clarity of objectives" (Neugebauer, 2008, p. 6).

Facilitating a Shared Program Vision and Mission

Because the program leader has the key role of "the keeper of the faith, the person who believes most deeply and cares most passionately for the central mission of the organization" (Neugebauer, 2000, p. 101), you have the responsibility for being the initial inspiration for your program's purpose. You take the lead in establishing and nurturing the program's vision, core values, and tone. However, as Margie Carter and Deb Curtis (2010) caution us, "A vision for an organization can't be just one person's idea" (p. 28).

While a vision statement expresses what you hope to accomplish, a mission statement describes the program's particular purpose and provides a framework for working toward the vision. They act as inspiration and guide for a program's work, laying the foundation for developing annual goals and educational objectives. Creating vision and mission statements that spell out your program's commitment to anti-bias education is a crucial step in beginning and then cultivating change.

For a vision to become more than a statement on a piece of paper, you must engage the interest and involvement of the program's key stakeholders in generating a shared vision and mission. The literature about best leadership practices agrees that facilitating the creation of a shared program vision and mission statement is fundamental (Bloom et al., 2010; Espinosa, 1997; Kagan & Neuman, 1997; G. Morgan, 2000; Neugebauer, 2000). To do this, collaborative leadership is essential.

In Chapter 4, we look at ways to engage your staff in developing an anti-bias vision and mission statement for your program and to review and possibly modify them in subsequent years. Even though you may feel ready to forge ahead alone, the time spent on creating a *shared* vision and mission for anti-bias work will be worth it in the long process of implementing change.

Establishing the Organizational Culture

A program's vision and mission statements become living documents when they are actively infused into all aspects of the program's organization, relationships, and practices. They are a "road map" (Neugebauer, 2008, p. 7) that helps guide the paths program leader and staffs take as they make choices about what they are doing. The leader also initiates a management system and an organizational culture that reflects the program's vision and mission statements (Carter & Curtis, 2010). Both the visionary and management sides of leadership are essential and "different sides of the same coin" (Bloom, 1997, p. 34).

A social–ecological perspective about organizational culture is well suited to its many-faceted relationships. In this approach, it is understood that each member of the community influences the collective values, mission, and style of the group's work. At the same time, the culture of the community shapes each member's attitudes and behavior. Therefore, a change in any component of the organization may affect all the others (Bloom et al., 2010; VanderVen, 2000). This perspective is also especially helpful for anti-bias education work.

According to P.J. Bloom and colleagues (2010), quality ECCE programs share certain central cultural and organizational characteristics including

- *Collegiality.* The staff feels a unified team spirit, collective sense of usefulness and effectiveness, and freedom to express their thoughts and to share information and resources. Conversations about values, beliefs, and educational priorities are normal parts of ongoing discussions.
- *Innovativeness.* Quality programs adapt to change and find creative ways to solve problems. This spirit of innovation doesn't just happen on its own; the program leader cultivates it. They "sense the need for change, set the pace for the change process, and monitor progress as new ideas are translated into action" (p. 19).
- *Professional growth.* Effective program leaders emphasize and provide ongoing opportunities for staff growth. This includes ways for staff to put new ideas into practice. Leaders also create a program climate that nurtures and stimulates the most skilled and dedicated staff, and mentor and coach those not yet performing as reliably. Multiple opportunities for growth take into account everyone's developmental journeys and life experiences.

Effective anti-bias programs establish and then build on these organizational dimensions of quality ECCE programs.

Supporting a Community of Learners

An active community of learners is the heart of building a quality ECCE program and culture of inquiry and adult learning. Creating an amiable place to work requires teachers balancing their time between working alone in their classrooms and spending time together reflecting about and improving their practice (Bloom et al., 2010). Through being members of a community of learners, staff have the opportunity to gain a deeper understanding of themselves, their relationships with each other, their work with children and families, and their knowledge of how children learn. Program leaders are both facilitators and members of this learning community. Multiple opportunities for growth take into account everyone's developmental journeys and life experiences (Bloom et al., 2010; Carter & Curtis, 2010; VanderVen, 2000).

Kugelmass (2004) describes how the teachers in a public elementary school came together with the school principal to "re-conceptualize their understanding of children and schooling" (p. 94). In interviews, teachers highlighted that ongoing, multiple ways to talk, learn, develop shared commitments, and make decisions together was central to promoting deep levels of cultural change.

Ongoing, facilitated conversation among staff is pivotal to flourishing learning communities. Some early childhood program leaders shy away from the conversations that anti-bias growth requires. Ellen Wolpert, an experienced anti-bias education leader, talks about ECCE directors asking her about how she keeps staff anti-bias conversations safe and comfortable. Her response illuminates one aspect of the perspective anti-bias program leaders need:

For me, the critical issue is how we encourage engagement in conversations that may sometimes be risky or uncomfortable. Comfort and safety mean very different things to people. Is this a concern about fear of disagreement, or conflict, or saying the wrong thing, or non-confidentiality, or realizing that someone is not like you? Some people want guarantees that their own definitions of safety and comfort will prevail, but we cannot guarantee that. Ground rules are useful, of course, such as establishing agreements about confidentiality and that people talk about their own experiences while also paying attention to a broader range of experiences that differ from their own. But beyond the ground rules, the task is being open to a new *kind* of conversation. (Personal communication, 2009)

Finding time in early childhood programs for staff to be a community of learners is another challenge, given the realities of insufficient staff and funding under which too many programs operate. Yet, as major contributors to our understanding of best ECCE leadership practices point out,

Even on a limited budget, there are many ways [to] increase opportunities for staff to expand their knowledge base and develop new skills and competencies. The amount of professional development activities in a program reflects leader priorities more than it does the level of financial resources. (Bloom et al., 2010, pp. 59–60)

Determined leaders find creative ways to carve out opportunities and time for staff members to meet often and regularly. For example, Chris Amirault, a director of a community-based center in an East Coast middle-sized city, solved the challenge of time for teachers to talk about anti-bias education in one ingenious way. He added a few hours per week to his budget for floating assistants to cover for his lead teachers. This allowed the teachers to meet every day for self-reflection and conversations with each other, about their anti-bias education work (personal communication, 2009).

Building Partnerships with Families

Respecting the centrality of the family's role in a child's life is an early, enduring ECCE principle. Gwen Morgan (2000) identifies related tasks such as being in regular communication with parents in ways that respect their values, and involving them in the life of the program. Similarly, the most recent revision of NAEYC's *Developmentally Appropriate Practice in Early Childhood Programs: Serving Children From Birth Through Age 8* states that "Mutual respect, cooperation, and shared responsibility inform the family–teacher relationships" (Copple & Bredekamp, 2009, p. 23).

Collaboration with families is also essential for meaningful anti-bias education (Derman-Sparks & Edwards, 2010; Derman-Sparks & Ramsey, 2011; Ramsey, 2004). As Lisa Lee, a leader in creating ECE programs that maintain collaborative partnerships with families eloquently explains,

Families honor us with the care of their children, . . . Instead of seeing "deficits" and cultural differences as the problem, teachers who are allies appreciate the strengths and "gifts" that families bring to the learning experience. When we bring depth to implementing an anti-bias approach, we uphold their trust . . . . What I learned from these relationships resulted in a shift in my perception of my role. Where once I benevolently helped families, who were appreciative in turn, I came to realize that I needed those families as much as they needed me. Where once I advocated on behalf of families, anti-bias work became about advocating together on things we both cared about on behalf of the children we cared so much about. (Quoted in Derman-Sparks & Edwards, 2010, p. 37)

Ongoing collaboration is how the leader and staff ensure that children's home cultures accurately become a central part of the daily life of the program. It also creates the environment in which it is possible to negotiate differences of ideas related to anti-bias concepts and activities. The leader provides professional development and encouragement for the staff to get to know the community and to make family life a central part of the classroom.

In spite of its importance, establishing collaborative partnerships with families is one area where many programs fall short. Neugebauer (2000) puts it plainly: "Conventional wisdom holds that child care is a partnership between parents and caregivers—parents and caregivers work hand-in-hand to meet the needs of the child. In reality, centers often do a less than adequate job in making the partnership work" (p. 102).

It is essential that program leaders find ways to address any anxieties that staff may feel about building partnerships with families. Providing opportunities for staff to increase their skills in working with families in general, and in relation to anti-bias issues, is part of the anti-bias program leader's responsibility for professional development (see Chapter 6 for ways to do this).

CORE ATTRIBUTES OF EFFECTIVE ECCE PROGRAM LEADERS

Leaders of early childhood care and education programs must have highly developed ability to interact with parents, staff, children, and community members and be able to tolerate the uncertainty and frustration that often come with these relationships.

Barbara Bowman (1997, p. 111)

The research and experiences of several leaders of the ECCE field point to a set of personal traits that support ECCE program leaders in meeting their multiple roles, tasks, and demands. These attributes are also necessary for effective anti-bias education leaders. Several of these traits are listed here:

- *Having the courage to lead.* This means understanding the risks and being aware of one's own fears, yet not letting fears prevent one from taking action (Espinosa, 1997).
- *Cultivating imagination.* This quality is "as critical to a program leader's success as acquiring skills" (Carter & Curtis, 2010, p. 3).
- *Willingness to engage in ongoing self-reflection and growth.* "A leader must be willing to examine her abilities and attitudes in order to positively influence the transformation of others. Every journey begins at home" (Espinosa, 1997, p. 101). Through ongoing reflective practice and continuing professional development, leaders create the core knowledge needed for their work (N. Brown & Manning, 2000).
- *Practicing what one preaches.* Leaders "push the what-is to the what-might-be—thinking possibility, invention, and vision" (Kagan & Neuman, 1997, p.60). And, they live their beliefs. As Zeece (2008) warns us, when program leaders set and enforce policy for staff, but disregard it themselves, "it fosters a sense of resentment and disrespect toward the director, and a sense of detachment from and disregard for the program and its goals" (p. 26).

- *Accepting and learning from mistakes.* Many scholars of best leadership practices talk about this trait. As Richard Clifford (1997) puts it, "leaders must not turn from failure but see the opportunity to learn from mistakes; this drive for the truth also means leaders welcome dissent and see it as means toward a more complete understanding" (p. 104).

- *Seeing "turbulence as an opportunity for positive change"* (VanderVen, 2000, p. 122). This attribute is especially important. Tension is often a sign that people really care about what's happening. When viewed this way, it becomes possible to move past discomfort and fear to a place of discovery and integrity (Carter & Curtis, 2010). Yet, handling staff disagreement and discomfort is problematic for many ECCE program leaders and teachers. Based on their studies of numerous ECCE programs, Bloom et al. (2010) cogently point out that

> The field of early care and education is filled with caring, compassionate people. And some of these people are just too caring, too compassionate, and too doggone nice. . . . They are squeamish about conflict and avoid it at all costs encounters . . . . Yet, highly charged differences of opinion are a normal and potentially healthy aspect of any workplace. (p. 48)

Leading effective anti-bias programs calls on people to overcome their discomfort with conflicts, as we discuss further in Chapter 7.

PROFESSIONAL DEVELOPMENT OF ECCE PROGRAM LEADERS

I did not know half of what I now know when I first started doing anti-bias education in the program I was directing. To build relationships with staff and families for doing anti-bias education, you have to do it and show that you mean it.

Ellen Wolpert (personal communication, 2009)

Effective ECCE program leaders need a broad knowledge base. Nancy Brown and James Manning (2000) suggest four essential areas, which serve as a useful framework for assessing what you already have in your repertoire and what you need to learn:

1. Reflective knowledge of self
2. Knowledge about others, including understanding how adults learn
3. Knowledge about how organizations work
4. Knowledge about the external world that surrounds the program.

In Chapter 3 we look at how these four types of knowledge come into play when program leaders "read" the context and dynamics of their programs before initiating anti-bias changes.

In her inventory of the necessary competencies of ECCE program administrators, Gwen Morgan (2000) adds knowing about current research findings in child and human development theory and their applicability to children's programs, concepts about caring, different supervisory styles and methods appropriate to a range of program staff, and different cultural styles of interacting. We add awareness of the research about young children's construction of identity and attitudes, as well as the mission, core learning goals, and basic pedagogical principles of anti-bias work (see Appendix A at www.tcpress.com for resources to strengthen your knowledge about anti-bias work). Additionally, embarking on the anti-bias development journey yourself will give you the understanding and empathy necessary for guiding the anti-bias journey of staff (see Chapter 1).

Growth in program leaders' core knowledge comes through reflective practice and continuing professional development (N. Brown & Manning, 2000). In addition to attending ECCE conferences and joining local directors' support groups, leaders should also participate in administrative training by organizations outside of the early childhood field. In order to develop the knowledge base needed for anti-bias work, leaders may need to access research and information from outside of ECCE in fields such as cultural studies and social justice, and in places like cultural centers and civil rights organizations.

Effective ECCE program leaders need ongoing connection with each other for mutual support, learning, and advocacy. "Your job can be much less stressful and much more rewarding, if you find ways to share, to communicate, to listen, to let off steam, to hear the steam of (your) colleagues, to join together to make much needed changes in public policy" (H. Morgan, 2008, p. 43). Participating in local support groups for ECCE program leaders and connecting with an experienced program leader are helpful ways to give and get support.

TAKING ON THE CHALLENGE

[The courage to lead] is born of the personal belief in the greater good benefiting all of us.

—Linda Espinosa (1997, p. 100)

Being the program leader of an early childhood program is never an easy task. Early childhood program leaders are expected to work in multiple, sometimes contradictory, roles. They are employer, guide, facilitator, boss, colleague, evaluator, and team member, as well as whatever else may need to be done to keep the program functioning economically and programmatically. An anti-bias education approach requires the courage to open oneself up to the complexities of diversity and equity issues—and to the conflict and growth the work brings. While empathizing with program leaders because of the challenges they face keeping a program on its feet, Carter and Curtis (2010) also urge them not to be overcome by those challenges:

It's easy for directors to feel helpless and victimized under conditions that include an ever-growing body of standards, required measureable outcomes, and a faltering economy. . . . While this feeling of helplessness is understandable, we also know that directors seldom claim the leadership potential their position offers them. Instead, they let the limitations and pressures of the current conditions constrict their imagination and creativity. . . . [They] tend to stay focused on how things are, rather than on a vision of how things could be. (p. 2)

Carter and Curtis conclude: "If you dare to take up a vision and not settle for the status quo, you are on the road to nurturing it into reality" (p. 114). Even with strong program leader practices, change can be difficult and frightening. It can also be exciting and enriching and, often, deeply satisfying.

In this chapter we laid out the best leadership approaches the early childhood care and education field has identified through experience and research. By incorporating these practices into your own leadership work, you can make your center a wonderful place for learning for *everyone*—even with all the difficult realities of early childhood conditions. These practices also provide a foundation for your journey to "shift the culture" of the program to an anti-bias education approach.

In the next chapters we relate ways to implement the central elements of effective ECCE program leadership and organizational culture, such as collaborative leadership, program vision and mission, organizational culture, a community of learners, and collaborative relationships with families. We begin in Chapter 3 by exploring the important process of "reading" your program as a place to start on this journey.

Reading the Program and Preparing for Anti-Bias Change

The anti-bias leader has clarity of stance. To be able to articulate this is what we are doing. This is what we believe in. This is who we are. This is what it's going to look like. It's not going to be easy. It is going to be uncomfortable at times, and sometimes you just need to sit with it. Not everything is solvable at first glance.

—Teacher

The commitment to build early childhood programs that embrace all children and families is the fuel of change. Leaders can make the most of this fuel through thoughtful, strategic planning and by skillfully guiding a program's organization, people, and culture. They identify what needs changing, manage the direction and rhythms of the change process, and monitor progress.

Being a strategic leader involves making decisions about where to put your energy, the speed at which to proceed, and what will be the most effective route to your goals and objectives. Doing this successfully requires you to gather information about the people and contexts of your program, and to consider how this portrait can guide you in developing strategies to meet anti-bias goals. Otherwise, you risk moving too fast and causing unnecessary problems or, conversely, underestimating the support for forging ahead and moving too slowly, or not at all.

Preparation for the long road toward greater equity and inclusion in your early childhood program begins with careful research. We use the metaphor of "reading" the program, adapted from Paulo Freire (1985), to describe the process of

1. Gathering a baseline understanding of your program's context
2. Analyzing this information for insights relevant to anti-bias change
3. Making preparations in response

We have also drawn on the antiracism work of the People's Institute for Survival and Beyond by adapting their "power analysis" process (Shapiro, 2002). In this kind of structural analysis, you identify the people, groups, and resources that could affect your program (as described later) and examine how they might support or oppose your work. This analysis enables you to look below the surface features of a program and determine who holds power over your program and who are the gatekeepers in your organization and community who can open or close doors to resources and support.

Early childhood programs are complex and dynamic systems consisting of different players, relationships, culture, and history. Reading your program will help you identify your community's assets, its challenges, and the key people who will be part of or affected by your anti-bias work. This includes identifying all the people and groups who affect your program both directly (e.g., staff and families) and indirectly (e.g., funding, licensing, accreditation). You need to understand who will benefit from an anti-bias approach, who is most likely to resist change, and who will be an ally in this work.

This chapter lays out a framework for establishing a preliminary or baseline understanding of the components of your program, and then discusses how to make sense of this information. Having a baseline will enable you to devise initial strategies to begin meeting your anti-bias goals. Finally, we suggest preparatory steps you can take based on your reading of the program. While this program reading, in full or in part, takes place in the first few months of the year (or whenever you initiate an anti-bias approach), you will return to this process periodically to assess progress and determine next steps (see Chapter 8). Given the demands of being a program leader, you will need to make choices about the time and energy that you can invest in this process. It is not necessary to complete all the detailed steps provided here in order to create change. Depending on your situation, you may decide to focus on certain aspects and spend less time on others. Balance the time spent on reading your program with taking action and learning from its outcomes.

COLLECTING PRELIMINARY IMPRESSIONS: ESTABLISHING A BASELINE FOR PLANNING

To make strategic choices about how to move forward on the anti-bias education journey, you should "read": (1) the physical and cultural landscape surrounding the program, (2) the program environment, (3) the program stakeholders, (4) the overall culture of the program, and (5) the program gatekeepers. Each of these components contributes to the initial portrait of your program's need and readiness for anti-bias work.

The Landscape

ECCE leaders tend to focus on what is happening within their centers, but anti-bias work requires a wider lens to include the broader cultural landscape surrounding the program. We have drawn on community-assets mapping as a tool for taking an inventory of the human and material resources, structures, and networks that exist for pursuing anti-bias goals (Kretzmann & McKnight, 1993). In addition, there are distinctive features of the surrounding community that may influence moving forward in this work.

Noteworthy elements of the landscape include:

- Ecological features of the program setting (e.g., rural or urban, on a military base, in an apartment complex)
- The demographics of families and staff in the program and in the neighboring community
- The social, cultural, and economic resources in the surrounding community and in the families' communities
- Important local issues, happenings, and politics of relevance to the program's anti-bias mission

Let us look at the contrasts in the cultural landscapes surrounding John's and Debbie's programs to demonstrate the importance of recognizing how differences might affect strategic choices. The cultural landscape of New Hampshire, where John's center is located, is very different from the context of Debbie's center in Massachusetts.

New Hampshire demographics are predominantly White and monocultural, with a relatively small, emerging group of residents who speak languages other than English. There is a large rural population, and significant pockets of poverty—much of which is rural. However, the closest neighborhood of the Child Study and Development Center (CSDC) is the surrounding university. It is a unique environment, with more ethnic and racial diversity than the state in general, although much of that diversity is from international students and staff. John arrived at a time when the university administration was articulating a clearer and stronger mission regarding diversity and equity. This move, including the appointment of a high-level position responsible for diversity matters, signaled institutional-level support for an anti-bias approach.

In contrast, the Eliot–Pearson Children's School (EPCS) in urban Medford, Massachusetts, presents a very different cultural landscape. The demographics are much more diverse than in New Hampshire across all social-identity categories. While the surrounding neighborhood reflects the upper-middle-class community of an elite private university, the children and families come from a broader cross-section of the Boston metropolitan area. Collectively, they reflect diversity in race, ethnicity, ability, family structure, and socioeconomic class. Both programs draw heavily from educated university communities and offer considerable resources, but Debbie's program includes staff, families, and community members with more experience living and working in diverse communities than in the relatively monocultural village of the public university in New Hampshire.

These contrasting social and cultural landscapes indicate the importance to anti-bias strategy of reading beyond the walls of the program. In John's program, socioeconomic class became a central aspect of identity exploration in his early anti-bias efforts. Debbie tapped into the diversity of her area to expand the school beyond its existing commitment to the inclusion of children with special needs. This meant actively recruiting families with varied racial and ethnic identities, as well as gay and lesbian families.

The Program Learning Environment

The physical environment of a program provides a stage for anti-bias education at the classroom level. You will need to document what resources already exist in the program and what you need to add. Broad questions include:

- Does the program have learning materials that accurately and respectfully reflect the backgrounds of the children and the people in their wider community?
- Does the program have resources for the staff (e.g., DVDs, books) about anti-bias education, social justice, and cultural awareness?
- Does the program have access to technology that could help in sharing and articulating the anti-bias mission?

Several anti-bias education resources offer specific suggestions for creating an inventory of the program environment (e.g., Derman-Sparks & Edwards, 2010, pp. 161–162; Ramsey, 2004, pp. 33–42). In Chapter 4 we discuss various strategies to involve staff in review of the program environment as part of their anti-bias professional development.

You should also consider other program environment factors that affect teachers' work in the classroom, such as the availability of time, space, and personnel. In addition, look at environmental factors that affect your efforts, such as professional development for teachers and supporting the specific needs of children and families. Ask questions such as the following:

- Do teachers have time and space to discuss anti-bias issues with colleagues, children, and families?
- Is personnel and program funding sufficient to enable teachers to carry out a quality program that meets diverse needs (e.g., providing books that reflect family diversity)?
- In what ways does the infrastructure of the facility support or restrain anti-bias efforts? For instance, the building or playground may or may not be accessible for children or adults with disabilities.
- Are there administrative policies and processes (e.g., admissions, tuition structure, communication methods) that could affect inclusion of families

of all backgrounds? For instance, some families may not have access to electronic communications.

The Stakeholders

The stakeholders include the individuals who actively participate in and have a direct investment in the success of your program. Each stakeholder may define program success differently, but the changes that come as you pursue an anti-bias mission will touch each of their lives in some way. They can potentially be a source of support or of opposition.

The following categories are the key stakeholder groups within ECCE programs and are the focus for this chapter:

- Program leader/s
- Teachers
- Families

While children are at the heart of your anti-bias efforts, the classroom teachers have primary responsibility for getting to know children in relation to anti-bias goals. At this point, you should take time to learn about the backgrounds of families and later assist teachers in their documentation and assessment of children's progress in anti-bias learning.

Depending on the structure of your program, you may have additional stakeholder groups with varying degrees of participation in the program and effect on anti-bias efforts. These groups include other program administrators and educators with leadership responsibilities, office personnel, interns and student teachers, volunteers, and auxiliary staff (e.g., cooks, custodians, and bus drivers). You should determine what you need to know about these groups and individuals as part of the preliminary read of the program. For instance, you may not be the supervisor for auxiliary staff members who enter the center after hours, but could be very reliant on their efforts.

To be an effective anti-bias leader, you need to get to know and build positive relationships with the members of all the stakeholder groups at your program. However, the dynamics and depth of the relationships with various stakeholders will vary. For example, teachers are employees and colleagues with whom you interact every day. In contrast, you see families less frequently and in a different professional role. As a result, you focus on collecting different kinds of information about each stakeholder group beginning with yourself as program leader.

Leader/s. You can generate a portrait of your anti-bias leadership capacity through self-reflection. The following questions are helpful in gauging one's readiness for leading anti-bias change:

- What is my leadership style? How do I make decisions and engage others in these decisions?
- What is my comfort level with risk taking and working through conflict with others?
- How do I view my social identity?
- What experience and knowledge do I have regarding anti-bias education?
- What are my values and long-terms goals for anti-bias education?

Teachers. These are the key players in implementing an anti-bias approach at the classroom level. In the roles of mentor and supervisor, you are in a unique position to learn about each teacher's readiness and get a sense of the group as a whole. You are looking for entry points to begin the process of change. For instance, if staff members have personal experience with diversity and bias, or are more familiar with the theory of oppression and privilege, you are likely to engage in a more challenging anti-bias dialogue. Try to get a preliminary read on the following:

- What is the teachers' awareness of their social and cultural identity (e.g., race, ethnicity, and social and economic class)?
- What interest and commitment do the teachers have in anti-bias values and goals?
- What is the teachers' capacity as advocates for an anti-bias approach? What are their relevant skills and experience?
- Which teachers could act as leaders or mentors to colleagues? Do those teachers have the respect of their peers due to experience or skills?

This preliminary read of the teachers' readiness for anti-bias education will primarily come from ongoing informal and formal conversations during supervision and meetings. You need to be intentional about raising anti-bias questions and conversation topics, and look for opportunities that arise. In reality, your impressions are likely to be very broad and tentative. Given the complexity of this work, it is important not to build rigid assumptions about teachers and to be open to new information.

Interviewing teachers about their hopes and dreams for the program is one specific tool to supplement informal information gathering. As you listen, look for key words and phrases that suggest awareness of social identity and potential interest in anti-bias goals, such *as privilege, culture, identity*, and *bias*. Teacher awareness may not be so explicit, so it is also important to listen carefully for language that shows an openness to diversity. The activities described in Chapter 4 provide further ways to read where teachers are at the beginning of school and throughout the year.

Families. Having a sense of where the children's families are in relation to anti-bias education is also helpful. While you may have a goal to know and connect with every family member, the depth of the relationships is likely to vary greatly and develop over time.

Beyond the general family demographic information (e.g., ethnicity, languages, family structure, and socioeconomic class) you collected as part of considering the landscape of the program, your reading of individual families is likely to be limited at this point. If you have been a member of the community for some time, you may have knowledge of families from your experiences. In addition, you are likely to get to know family members on the governing board or advisory committee because you are involved in early discussions about philosophy, curriculum, personnel, and funding.

Later in this chapter, we share the process of identifying family members who may be potential allies for your anti-bias mission. You may also get indicators of families who may have concerns or objections to anti-bias values. As with the teachers, you should be wary of early impressions that often converge on extremes of support or potential opposition. Be open to a more complex understanding of families and their perspectives. In Chapter 5 we explore the long-term process of getting to know families during their time at the program in order to develop a partnership in this work.

The Culture of the Program

Effective early childhood leaders understand that their program has a dynamic culture that is responsive to both the people in the program and its history (Greenman, 1995). When we talk about anti-bias education involving a shift in the culture of a program (to one that is more inclusive), we are using the term *culture* broadly to describe the program's values, rules, and practices.

Like an anthropologist, a leader who is new to a program can often observe and identify the culture more easily than someone who has been immersed in its daily life over time. If you have been at a center for many years, you will have to make a conscious effort to step outside of the culture and take a fresh look at it, given that you have been a participant and contributor. All of the program components we have identified for information gathering (landscape, learning environment, and stakeholders) are part of the culture of your program. In addition, the following are some important elements to look for:

- Staff power dynamics: Who are the people who tend to speak up, attend events, and participate in committees and other decision-making bodies?
- What are the formal policies, typically in staff and family handbooks?
- What are the implicit rules and language that the community has passed down orally over time?
- What are the key rituals and traditions in the program community?

This information is important to anti-bias change for a couple of reasons. First, you will discover which individuals and groups appear excluded or less visible in the program, as well as which ones seem to hold more power and influence. In addition, implicit (informal) rules often reflect important but unexamined values that long-term staff and families have accepted as set in stone. For instance, community members may assume that male teachers would never work in the infant classroom. With awareness of the program's culture, you can avoid harmful mistakes by building trust, awareness, and buy-in before questioning or nixing much-loved traditions that may not be inclusive (e.g., an annual holiday carnival).

Gatekeepers

Gatekeepers are people or groups that have power over a program's operations by virtue of their institutional position and role. They may control access to people, resources, and knowledge, and create regulations that are relevant to anti-bias efforts. Potential gatekeepers include oversight organizations and funders (e.g., governing board, foundations), various regulatory groups, the school district, and town council. Leaders themselves also act as gatekeepers.

An anti-bias leader looks carefully at these gatekeeper roles and works creatively to minimize the obstacles. Later in this chapter, we consider the possibility of gatekeepers acting as allies and resources. Here are some of the questions you might consider regarding gatekeepers, depending on your particular circumstances:

- Does the administrative entity that oversees your program (e.g., board, school district, agency) have any written criteria, standards, or policies that can support your anti-bias education efforts?
- Does the program depend on funders for support of operations and capital projects (e.g., to make the playground accessible to children and adults with disabilities)?
- Does the building owner have particular values with regard to diversity that might align or contrast with anti-bias values? For example, a religious organization that owns a facility may insist on adherence to values that support or conflict with anti-bias education.
- What items in the applicable regulations (e.g., licensing and accreditation criteria, building code) might support or interfere with your anti-bias work?

Leaders as Gatekeepers. As a program leader, you play a gatekeeper role in terms of admissions, hiring, policy development, and budgeting. By looking critically at these administrative structures, you can identify ways to remove obstacles. For example, you can open the "gate" into the program by being proactive in seeking more diversity in admissions or by prioritizing anti-bias skills and experiences in your staff hiring process.

Oversight Bodies. There may be individuals and organizations that have varying degrees of oversight responsibility for your program's operations. These include community and institutional groups such as religious and social service agencies that act as umbrella organizations for an ECCE program. A nonprofit program has a board that makes decisions regarding policy, budget, and personnel, while Head Start and other government-funded programs are accountable to advisory groups or to school, district, state, and federal personnel. Campus-based programs at higher education institutions typically report to a college department, consisting of faculty and other administrators.

In addition, you need to consider the various funders (e.g., individuals, foundations, government) that, while not directly involved in program oversight, may be important contributors to your annual budget or specific capital projects. In particular, you need to know if an anti-bias initiative could jeopardize funding, or conversely, if there are organizations that might be particularly interested in financially supporting such efforts.

Regulators. Licensing, accreditation, and other regulatory bodies (e.g., local council, state, federal) are the most visible gatekeepers for early childhood programs. These requirements create boundaries (some real, some imagined) that can get in the way of innovative anti-bias efforts. Some programs may also be subject to local building code regulations or even insurance requirements that could affect operations.

Because of their role in interpreting and enforcing rules, those who monitor your compliance with licensing can make your life difficult around anti-bias efforts. Licensors can also prove to be important sources of support. We have found it useful to find out your licensor's understanding of and commitment to anti-bias education up front and to figure this information into how you approach anti-bias issues that arise.

Regulations are a source of support and obstacles to anti-bias work. NAEYC's *Code of Ethical Conduct and Statement of Commitment* (NAEYC, 2011) and *Early Childhood Program Standards and Accreditation Criteria: The Mark of Quality in Early Childhood Education* (NAEYC, 2007) stipulate that diversity work is an important element of early childhood programs. On the other hand, licensing criteria can get in the way. For instance, the health requirement that children wash their hands on arrival can send a mixed message to families you are also trying to welcome. An anti-bias program leader seeks to negotiate a constructive and reasonable solution to these issues. For example, a licensing requirement that infants sleep in individual cribs, clashed with a family's cultural use of a hammock at home. The approved solution was to hang the hammock diagonally inside the crib at the center (Derman-Sparks & Edwards, 2010). Later in this chapter we discuss the possibility that regulations and those responsible for them can be allies.

MAKING SENSE OF THE BASELINE FOR STRATEGIC PLANNING

In this phase of reading a program, you carefully consider the meaning of the baseline information that has been collected about the landscape, learning environment, stakeholders, gatekeepers, and program culture. By taking stock of the anti-bias readiness of key stakeholders, and identifying potential allies, opportunities, and obstacles, you can generate informed initial strategies for embarking on anti-bias action. As you start carrying out your initial strategies, you will continue to evaluate the outcomes and make new plans accordingly.

Take Stock: Readiness, Opportunities, and Obstacles

At this point, you have inventoried the features and resources of the program environment and surrounding landscape, developed a preliminary understanding of key stakeholders, and formed a broad understanding of the program culture. Next you should focus on the task of figuring out the readiness of yourself, the teachers, and overall program and community to engage in anti-bias action. Then you can consider the potential opportunities and obstacles to the anti-bias mission.

An *opportunity* is any factor that has the potential to fuel your program's anti-bias mission. You can identify and activate the opportunity. In contrast, an *obstacle* is a factor that can slow, complicate, or even stall your shifting of the program culture. You can mitigate, reframe, or eliminate obstacles through creative problem solving, or by adjusting plans and goals. For instance, lack of funding can limit the materials for anti-bias efforts (e.g., purchasing persona dolls for anti-bias story telling). Thinking creatively, you could reframe the situation as an opportunity to bring staff, families, and community members together to raise funds or to make learning materials. This deliberative process of recognizing opportunities and obstacles helps you feel empowered rather than overwhelmed or ambushed by the challenges of anti-bias work.

Leader Readiness. Regardless of commitment to an anti-bias approach, each leader brings very different skills, knowledge, experience, and awareness to the task. For instance, a leader may feel comfortable in moving forward with discussions and training related to social and economic class in part because of growing up in a working class family (opportunity). In contrast, the same leader may feel very uncertain about supporting families around international adoption without taking time to do some reading first (obstacle).

Knowing your capacity for anti-bias work will help you understand the strengths you bring to implementing anti-bias values (opportunities), as well where you need to grow (obstacles). For instance, a leader's fears and uncertainties can be an obstacle to taking the risks needed for this work. With self-awareness and support from colleagues, you can turn fears into opportunities for growth. Debbie's and John's backgrounds provide relevant examples. Debbie points out her strengths and challenges:

As a woman of color, I had a life history that helped me have a realistic view of how racism operates and understand the urgency of seeking broad inclusion. On the flip side, I am very conscious of not having teachers see me as the go-to person on Chinese culture. As a leader, I was organized and hands on—strengths I harnessed in my work with staff. With such a passionate anti-bias vision, my challenge at times was to know when to let go and allow teachers to make mistakes.

John contrasts his own style to Debbie's:

I am very aware of my cautious personal style, which both supported my strategic thinking and challenged my willingness to take risks. I also crossed gender-role norms by being a man in the field of early education; this offered me a unique insight into the challenges for boys in developing a healthy gender identity.

Leaders are also intentional about how they articulate, and when they share, their anti-bias commitment with others. For instance, John recalls:

At my first annual goal-setting meeting at the center, I decided to share my goal broadly as "Explore and implement strategies for expanding the social and cultural diversity of the curriculum, pedagogy, and community." I chose this approach because I did not see explicit anti-bias goals coming directly from individual meetings with teachers. By articulating a broad goal, I hoped that most staff would feel included in the dialogue and action of the first year.

These kinds of choices require that leaders have clarity about their anti-bias strategy.

The leader's history in a program is an important consideration in how to proceed with anti-bias efforts. For instance, when you are new to a program, there is often an expectation that you will make substantive changes in policy and practice (opportunity). At the same time, it is important to take time to observe the culture of the program and its context. If you are an experienced leader, especially one who has been at the program for years, you probably have established a good deal of trust and social capital within the community (opportunity). Teachers and families are less likely to question your motives and competence in initiating change. The respectful relationships built over time will have a positive effect on any conflicts encountered.

Finally, a leader's energy and workload are important elements of readiness. It is crucial to acknowledge that there are many demands on you—from problem solving to meet the needs of staff and families, paying attention to regulations and standards, and creating and managing the budget, to evaluating staff, dealing with the facility, and building relationships in the larger community. Although anti-bias education is not a separate part of the curriculum, but rather integrated into everything you do, it still requires your time and conscious effort. Conversely, this work can energize you and the teachers because of the creativity, emotional investment, and connection to deep values that it entails.

Teacher Readiness. The leader seeks to uncover where each teacher is in understanding and experience with anti-bias education. Everyone is going to experience some resistance and discomfort as anti-bias changes occur and the culture of the program begins to shift to a many-cultures perspective. However, you can more effectively move the work forward by carefully reading where people are on their anti-bias journey and responding with thoughtful scaffolding and strategizing.

Drawing on the adult developmental framework presented in Chapter 1, you can construct a general awareness of where teachers initially fit in this framework as individuals and as a staff. The following broad categories are useful as starting points, but your first impressions of teachers are likely to be incomplete.

- *Resistant:* The teacher seems uncomfortable talking about diversity, talks or acts in discriminatory ways, and/or has expressed objections to an anti-bias approach (e.g., a teacher complains about a Bhutanese family using their home language at the center).
- *Beginner:* The teacher seems unaware of or has little experience with different social identities. You may see a differences-denial approach of "we are all the same" (e.g., when observing in a classroom, you notice that a teacher ignores a child who asks, "How come Eliza smells funny?").
- *Learner:* The teacher is open to talking and thinking about diversity and is willing to take on new challenges. This teacher may already be using aspects of an anti-bias approach in the classroom but does not take an activist stance (e.g., you observe children playing with dolls of different skin colors).
- *Mentor:* The teacher has expertise and experience in anti-bias education, professionally and/or personally. These teachers will be important allies in moving forward with change (e.g., the teacher offers suggestions about how to ensure the upcoming harvest festival is accessible to families of all socioeconomic backgrounds).

One factor that can affect where teachers are in their developmental journey is their history in the program. Veteran teachers may be comfortable with the status quo and resist change (obstacle), while newer teachers may be more open to trying an anti-bias approach (opportunity). Over the long-term, high teacher turnover can become an obstacle because it makes it difficult for a leader to gear training and expectations to varying levels of familiarity with an anti-bias approach. In these situations the leader will draw more heavily on teachers viewed as potential mentors of their peers (opportunity).

Program and Community Readiness. Look for the aspects of diversity that are meaningful to the key stakeholders in the program in the context of their backgrounds and the philosophy and traditions of the program. Consider how these factors might help people make a connection to anti-bias values and issues. For example, John describes a surprising discovery at CSDC:

While nearly all of the families spoke English, I found that 25% of the families spoke more than one language at home. As a result, a workshop on dual-language learning proved very popular and led to a parent-facilitated, follow-up dialogue. This, in turn, led to recommendations for changes in the children's curriculum and the program.

The community landscape also presents potential opportunities and obstacles in relation to bias and equity issues. Knowing these helps avoid unwelcome surprises and increases the possibilities for networking with allies in the community. For instance, the town mayor and police chief are hosting a neighborhood barbeque to create greater connection between residents and newly arrived families with refugee status (opportunity). On the flip side, some in the community may be campaigning through the local media to retain traditional Christmas celebrations in public programs for children (obstacle).

The program leader must consider the possibility of opposition to anti-bias efforts from people in the larger community. For example, in Chapter 7 we look at a community where there was an attempt to stop an ECCE program from including children's books and posters showing two mothers or fathers. This speaks to the need for program leaders to move strategically and to be aware that, sadly, social justice values continue to be controversial in many places. Most leaders and programs will not have to face this kind of obstacle. However, it is wise to not be naive and unprepared and to be aware that some kind of external opposition is possible.

Identify Potential Allies

An *ally* is a person or group who shares and strives to implement your anti-bias values, supports and publically endorses your anti-bias efforts, understands the challenges involved in the work, and provides access to resources and networks. As they develop their anti-bias understanding and skill, some allies become true collaborators and take on leadership tasks.

You should identify allies and their potential to contribute individually and institutionally to your anti-bias efforts to shift the culture of the program. An ally has one or more of the following characteristics:

1. Seems open to new ideas
2. Asks thoughtful questions about bias, equity, and diversity
3. Indicates willingness to take risks in supporting anti-bias values
4. Has personal experience or social identity outside mainstream culture
5. Demonstrates experience and expertise relevant to anti-bias education

Building relationships with individuals in the various stakeholder and wider circles is central to finding allies. This work does not happen overnight. It means being observant and being ready to take advantage of opportunities that arise.

A program leader's immediate allies come from staff and families. However, not all stakeholders are allies, and not all allies are stakeholders. They also come from the program's gatekeepers and from the leader's network of community and professional colleagues. While gatekeepers and community groups are more distant from the daily work of a program, they can play significant ally roles, such as being conduits to a range of resources.

Staff Allies. Pay attention to signs of staff members' interest in, explicit support for, and willingness to implement anti-bias education. Another indicator of their anti-bias commitment is holding themselves and their colleagues accountable to anti-bias values. Some staff members may have personal experiences with diversity and bias, or may have knowledge about issues such as cultural relevancy, social justice, or children's identity development. These qualities all provide useful entry points for anti-bias initiatives.

Signs of potential allies appear during everyday discussions, in supervision sessions, in staff meetings and workshops, and in annual survey comments. You can encourage these signs by responding positively when a staff member makes a suggestion related to the anti-bias mission. For example, John recalls:

A teacher at the center proposed that the entire staff read a book she had found insightful about examining the discomfort that often comes with social justice work [Jacobson, 2003]. While not necessarily the book I would have chosen at that time, I decided it was important to act on this opening from the teacher and for the staff to read something recommended by a colleague.

Another approach to uncovering allies is to initiate a voluntary staff anti-bias taskforce or discussion group that meets after hours. While this strategy does not guarantee that all the participating teachers will be effective allies, and may exclude interested staff who cannot attend for family reasons, it is one way to help gauge interest and commitment.

Family Allies. Family members make powerful allies because they have a voice as program clients and are in a position to have expectations of the program. Unlike the teachers and program leader, they are not responsible for providing a service to other families and are not constrained by professional boundaries. For example, a parent or guardian can speak up compellingly in a family workshop about personal experiences with racism without being as concerned about offending others or revealing too much confidential information. John notes, "I found that a parent ally request or complaint related to anti-bias values could relieve me from always having to be the one setting expectations for staff." However, since families are clients, you should also pay attention to professional boundaries that may limit your personal connection with a parent ally. It is important that you do not give special attention to particular families just because they are avid anti-bias supporters.

Indicators of potential allies among the children's families come during both one-on-one and group meetings. The intake interview at the beginning of a family's entrance into the program is one opportunity to gauge interest. Pay attention to specific experiences and expertise that family members have with diversity and social justice issues. For instance, you could discover that a family member is an advocate for refugee and migrant rights at a local legal office.

Test the waters by inviting parents and guardians to join hiring and other committees and see how they respond to discussions related to anti-bias goals. For example, a parent member of a hiring committee might express concern about a job applicant's lack of experience with family diversity. Emails are another source of evidence, such as when a family in John's program emailed him their concern about the lack of teachers reflecting the different cultural groups in the center.

ECCE Colleagues as Allies. Building relationships with other ECCE directors and programs that share a commitment to anti-bias education is also vital. Attending local director support groups and participation in local and state committees of professional organizations are ways to locate allies. These colleagues may be at different phases in their own understanding and practice of anti-bias education, but may still offer significant support. Attending conference workshops about diversity and equity work is another opportunity to identify professional allies.

ECCE colleague allies offer support in multiple ways. First, you can share experiences and ideas, as well as access new strategies and activities. Second, you can think and problem-solve difficult issues with colleagues in person and through email, Skype™, and social media. A third benefit of networking is getting emotional support and friendly reality checks. The stress and complexity of anti-bias leadership can wear you down. Leaders periodically need to unload and check in with colleagues who have similar values and responsibilities. Finally, you can collaborate with other program leaders on professional development opportunities in order to share trainer costs and connect your teachers to staff from different cultural contexts.

Community Groups and Networks. Community, state, and national advocacy groups outside of the ECCE field that focus on identity, diversity, and social justice issues are another potential source of ally support. They have relevant information, resources, and experiences, and can help with problem solving and strategies. For instance, a local bookstore owner could provide you with access to used books to borrow for staff professional development on gender issues. At another program, a relationship with a Latino community center might provide access to Spanish translation services and information on local cultural celebrations. Another illustration comes from John's experience in a university setting:

Through a relationship with an ally on a university-wide diversity team, we organized a meeting at the center with her and the head of the office for student diversity affairs. They helped us brainstorm events on campus that would be appropriate venues for families and children to interact with a diverse group of adults. We discussed a wheelchair basketball tournament, various holiday celebrations (e.g., Divali), and the idea of classrooms attending a rehearsal of the annual Black Student Union fashion show so children could provide feedback.

Some social service organizations have conferences where ECCE people can meet professionals from other professional fields who may become allies. For example, Louise reaped valuable knowledge and encouragement over the years through her relationship with the national antiracism educational and organizing group Crossroads Ministry, which is an interfaith group working on social justice.

Gatekeepers as Allies. One of the most strategic and difficult places to identify allies is among people who have power and authority over the program or in the community. While ECCE program leaders have considerable power to make decisions independently, many are typically accountable to a higher authority. This could include the director of the agency that oversees the program, a district superintendent, or a college dean. In some cases, the people acting as gatekeepers are not early childhood professionals, but come from other social service backgrounds or other professional roles (e.g., business manager).

Even though they are not always in direct or regular contact with the program, the people in these positions can be valuable as allies because of the power they have in relation to funding, public relations, and policy. It is important for you to be intentional about developing relationships and finding opportunities to share the program's anti-bias education goals and efforts. For instance, a board member for a community child-care program shows interest in the program leader's collaboration with a community garden, which is growing vegetables for a local food pantry. Realizing that the board member might share the program's social justice values, the leader invites her to be part of a meeting to discuss plans to engage the children in the project. Later, the board member's support proves helpful in locating funding for new garden beds and in securing city council approval.

Regulators (and regulations) are gatekeepers that can also be allies in your work. Accreditation typically includes explicit criteria that support both cultural relevancy and anti-bias education in the program and classroom. For instance, a quick search of the NAEYC (n.d.) online accreditation TORCH site using the term *bias* came up with the following statement:

> The criteria are designed to be inclusive of all children, regardless of ability, culture, language, ethnicity, religion, or socioeconomic status. Teachers are expected to counter potential bias and discrimination (1.D.01 and 3.B.04) and to help children build their understanding of diversity. (2.L.03)

As the leader, you have a responsibility to be aware of these criteria and use the language to promote anti-bias efforts with staff and families. With some creativity and relationship building with gatekeepers, you can often find constructive solutions to apparent obstacles. To illustrate this point, John recounts the following story:

> I had been encouraging teachers to take children on field trips into the local community as a way to increase their access to more diversity and potential anti-bias curriculum. Families, staff, and students often used the university's shuttle bus service to visit various places on and near campus. Unfortunately, the state licensing regulations dictated that a child under kindergarten age could not be on a bus without a safety belt and car seat. I talked with the head of licensing, someone I regarded as an ally through our membership on a child-care taskforce, and pointed out that children in the city ride public transportation every day. She advised us to appeal through the formal process and subsequently granted us a variation on our license for younger children to ride the bus with parent permission.

SETTING THE STAGE FOR ACTION

In this chapter we have provided examples of how reading the program can help with generating thoughtful strategies for anti-bias action. You can also take some beginning steps that help get the ball rolling or set the stage for the long term.

Adjust the Program Structures

Policies and Procedures. Creating program policies that affect staff and families is one of the program leader's core responsibilities. After reviewing formal policies (typically in handbooks), you can make immediate changes to policies that present obstacles to anti-bias goals and add some that proactively support them. The policy (and practice) regarding holiday celebrations is often one that requires rethinking.

This step would also include a review of administrative paperwork to ensure that it is inclusive of all families. One example is the application and intake forms that include spaces for mother and father, rather than being inclusive of the range of family structures. Another possibility is to have dual-language forms for families who are more comfortable using their home language.

It is important for you to recognize that policies—whether formalized in print or informal based on tradition—are not written in stone, and you can rethink, modify, or eliminate them. You must also decide whether to simply change the policy or go through a slower process of discussion with staff and families to arrive at a more helpful policy. The choice depends on an analysis of priorities: Is this a straightforward or urgent change that needs to happen quickly (e.g., the application form), or is this a complex issue that presents an opportunity for engaging stakeholders in a learning process that leads to a sense of ownership (e.g., holiday policy)?

Admissions Priorities. After reviewing the program demographics, you may decide to be more proactive in seeking families and children with particular backgrounds and identities. To change admissions for the following year, prior planning is necessary. You may have the authority to adjust policies and forms to reflect priorities, or you could focus on community outreach to increase the diversity of child and family backgrounds in your applications. John reports:

I worked with the parent advisory committee to include specific language that identified increasing the diversity of family backgrounds as an admissions priority. I also found that I was able to create small shifts in the demographics of the families by eliminating or limiting policies such as alumni and sibling priorities for new spaces.

Debbie points out, "I redesigned the school brochure to make it more accessible in language and format (e.g., adding more images and less text)." Both John and Debbie also undertook targeted outreach to local religious and community organizations with populations that might increase diversity of family backgrounds.

Budget Allocations. While we believe it is possible to implement anti-bias education within any budget, the allocation of funds does reflect the program's priorities. Program leaders have varying degrees of decision-making power over the annual budget and the funding of specific components, with some having full jurisdiction over it. However, even when they share budget decision making with oversight administrators or agencies, leaders typically have the ability to make small but important changes in the distribution to specific budget items.

For instance, you can decide to make sure that there are funds for immediately expanding anti-bias learning materials. As needs get identified, it may be useful to decide to dedicate most of your classroom materials budget one year to a particular aspect of anti-bias work, such as ensuring that all classrooms have books reflecting all the home languages spoken by families or sending a classroom team to an anti-bias training program.

While some budget changes can happen immediately, others require long-term planning—maybe over a number of years. The leader is involved in making the case for the expenditures and seeking even incremental changes each year. For instance, the leader may be able to adjust how tuition is structured (and create a sliding scale as is the case in John's program), or build a scholarship fund (as Debbie was able to do in part by instituting a new application fee).

Hiring Procedures. A staff that comes from diverse backgrounds and has the capacity and commitment to support anti-bias education is vital. These qualities become part of the criteria for selecting new teachers so that candidates have clarity about the program's values. Because openings can arise at any time, you need to develop a plan early on that includes hiring practices that can attract a diverse pool of candidates (e.g., proactive outreach into specific communities or community-based advertising media), and meets specific program needs (e.g., teachers who speak languages other than English). Selecting diverse hiring committees and including specific interview questions about diversity and equity also improve anti-bias hiring. Possible interview questions include the following:

- Give an example from your experience of figuring out a difference between a parent's views and your own beliefs or program policies. What did you do, and what guided your choices about how to respond?
- We work hard to make sure that our programs are comfortable places for children and families of different cultural backgrounds. What are some examples from your own experience of things you have done to ensure a welcoming environment?
- If you hear a child make a comment to another child that rejects some aspect of the child's identity, what would you do?

Prepare Yourself

As a leader, you also change yourself. Having assessed your own readiness for the journey ahead, you should develop a plan for professional growth. You may need to do further reading and learning about the adult anti-bias developmental stages or about implementing anti-bias work with children. You may decide you need to learn more about facilitating anti-bias discussions (see the resource list and strategies in Appendix A, online at www.tcpress.com).

While leadership is vital, you will not be doing this work by yourself; progress does not just depend on you alone. As you generate a plan for preparing yourself, it is also important to have collaborators on the journey ahead. As discussed in the section on identifying allies, you will find support from both within and outside your program. Identify them as early as possible, and do not be shy about asking for help.

Leadership is a strategic balance between what you want to accomplish and what you can actually do. You seek to do what is "within your reach and within your power." Shifting the culture of your program to an anti-bias community requires a mix of thoughtful pragmatism (What is happening here? What is our capacity?) and visionary optimism (We will get there! It is possible!).

A DYNAMIC AND CYCLICAL PROCESS

The aim of an anti-bias leader is to realize deep and lasting change in all the components of the program. This does not happen quickly. While a long-term view of change is often in tension with the urgency of social justice (When do we want it? Now!), we believe such a view is essential to shifting the culture of a program.

Reading the program is a preliminary step, as well as a dynamic, cyclical process. Using the initial read as a preliminary baseline, you can begin to act. Throughout the year, you should periodically revisit what you know and assess what is happening. Based on the analysis at each point, you can develop a new set of strategies to meet anti-bias goals.

We now turn to the specific strategies and activities for working with teachers (Chapters 4 and 6) and families (Chapter 5) over the long haul of the anti-bias journey.

CHAPTER 4

Fostering Reflective Anti-Bias Educators

First and foremost, the leader needs to be deeply invested in this work. He then needs to present it to the staff as an invitation to explore issues of diversity and be sure there is time and opportunity for staff to be engaged.

—Teacher

Becoming skilled at anti-bias education in the classroom is an ongoing journey, that calls on educators to engage in a cycle of practice and reflection about themselves and their actions. They must do much more than acquire a few new materials or develop new activities. Anti-bias education cannot be mastered in a one-time workshop or by reading a book. Most teachers largely learn how to do ABE on the job, in specific settings with specific children and families.

Anti-bias leaders provide the necessary time, space, resources, support, and facilitation for teachers and other staff to be part of the process of change. They build a community of learners that enables everyone to explore and grapple with anti-bias issues. A collaborative style of leadership, the preferred early childhood education model, empowers staff members to first begin and then take ownership of their anti-bias work.

All early childhood programs have a staff with a range of awareness, interest, and experiences with diversity and anti-bias education. Some staff members are new to diversity work; others have experience doing some type of diversity and anti-bias work in their previous training or classrooms or have been exploring their own issues of identity. Some may have more experience than the program leader; others may resist an anti-bias approach. As the program leader, your charge is to find ways to provide a variety of learning opportunities for all of the staff, given their diverse range of awareness, interest, and experiences. You should scaffold the anti-bias education growth of the individual staff members, as well as the movement of the group as a whole.

This chapter offers a range of strategies and activity examples, organized in two main sections. First, we describe ways to build the community of anti-bias learners. Second, we offer strategies for engaging staff in learning about and starting to implement an anti-bias education framework. Throughout this chapter, as well as subsequent ones, composite quotes from teachers and parents at EPCS and CSDC are used to introduce the various sections.

All activities work for teachers at any stage in their anti-bias journey; keep in mind where they are developmentally. Drawing from a constructivist framework, we assume that, as with children, teachers at different places in their development will engage with and take away different lessons from the same learning experience. For this reason it is effective to revisit activities you have previously implemented. Similarly, as with children, strive to match the needs of those you are teaching, rather than assuming that any specific activity is the best way to teach a particular topic or content. All the strategies and activities are applicable to teachers; most may also be used with the entire staff (see the definition in Figure I.1 in the Introduction). Resources for further activity ideas are available in our online Appendix A at www.tcpress.com.

BUILDING A COMMUNITY OF ANTI-BIAS LEARNERS

When we put effort and care into anti-bias education, we see and feel it throughout the entire school.

—Teacher

Anti-bias work grows best in an environment where collegial, mutually respectful relationships among staff and between staff and the program leader are the norm and where a culture exists that fosters open conversation and dialogue, reflection, and risk taking.

The goal is to create a caring and welcoming environment in which staff feel respected and trusted from the very first day. As pointed out in Chapter 2, this is a central tenet of effective program leadership in ECCE, and many resources already exist that offer strategies for creating collegial relationships. Here are strategies for establishing and deepening anti-bias culture and interactions.

Create a Climate for Taking Risks

I've learned anti-bias education is messy work; you [the director] have given us permission to make mistakes. I know you've got my back especially when I am trying things that I don't always feel comfortable with!

—Teacher

Once you lay a foundation of mutually respectful relations with staff, it is time to begin engaging teachers in reflection and conversations about their identity, their biases, and anti-bias issues. These conversations inevitably lead to personal disclosure that feels risky and uncomfortable at different times. Some teachers embrace the opportunity to stretch their thinking and consider new perspectives. Others feel unsettled by the disequilibrium they experience as they gain better self-understanding, uncover biased attitudes, and encounter challenges to their worldviews. People experience embarrassment or guilt about their lack of awareness and role in perpetuating bias. They also feel anger and pain as they reveal hurtful experiences in their lives. In these situations adults confuse feeling discomfort with being unsafe. These are not the same dynamics.

Constructivist theory tells us that if people feel supported in their learning, disequilibrium and its accompanying discomfort can lead to growth. Everyone deserves to engage in a dialogue with their colleagues where they feel emotionally safe and respected. As the program leader, you have the responsibility to create a climate for discussions in which participants will not feel under attack. At the same time, you must help everyone to understand that feeling discomfort is a part of the anti-bias journey. Avoiding uncomfortable conversations does not lead to growth. It simply results in keeping things as they are, rather than creating new perspectives and practices. In Chapter 7 we focus in on the central role of conflict in anti-bias change.

Setting Ground Rules. Agreeing upon and practicing ground rules help create a safe environment for open anti-bias discussions. Doing so establishes the norms of interaction from the very beginning of the school year. Parker Palmer (1997) refers to two kinds of norms as a useful framework. *Structural norms* define when, where, and how long staff meetings will take place and rules for the conversation, such as maintaining confidentiality, active listening, and respecting silence. *Interpersonal norms* are those that allow a group to feel safe, such as speaking from one's own experiences, suspending judgment of others' narratives, being honest, and assuming goodwill. At the first staff meeting of the year, you should engage everyone in setting the ground-rule norms, brainstorming the question, "What do I need to do my best work?" Revisit these ground rules periodically at subsequent meetings, and change or add additional ones as needed.

Modeling Leader Risk Taking. When program leaders model risk taking around anti-bias topics, they encourage staff to go beyond their comfort zone and risk opening themselves to new ideas and ways of working with each other, families, and children. As the program leader, you can model risk taking by acknowledging and doing something that is uncomfortable for you, sharing mistakes you have made as leader, and acknowledging that you don't know all the answers. As one teacher at the EPCS explained to Debbie:

The director needs to model anti-bias education. You share a lot of your experiences with us, your messiness is public, you make very clear what the stance and the expectations are for teachers, for parents, for kids. Then you have our backs when conflicts come up: that is really important.

John also relates an example about modeling taking risks:

At one of our staff retreats, I talked about my experience as a man in early childhood, a young teacher in a profession in which there are very few men. I found that one of the very early questions from interview committees (made up of parents) was about my policy regarding giving children affection. I didn't recognize it at first – but, in retrospect, I realize there was an underlying homophobic agenda. My female colleagues weren't getting the same questions. I also discovered that a dad on one committee, a professional in the legal system, ran a criminal background check on me—this was many years before these checks were the norm. Sharing this information with my staff as their director was *very* personal and somewhat emotional. People listened intently. I have always felt it is important for the leader to be a participant with the staff as well as share your expertise.

Educators Supporting Each Other. Eric Hoffman describes an additional central technique for creating a learning community where teachers feel supported to meet the challenges of anti-bias work. He works hard to facilitate teachers identifying the places where they need support from teammates and from the program leader. They discuss what issues each teacher feels able to handle with families and where each needs someone to step in. He also talks about who is most suited to step in, depending on the situation or issue. He notes that the need does not arise very often, but for the teachers, knowing that they are each other's allies makes it easier to handle difficult situations. Everyone feels supported (personal communications, 2010).

In the next two sections are activities and strategies to use with staff in the beginning of the school year. The first category of activities is about getting to know each other and our multiple identities. The second category of activities is about understanding anti-bias education. You can use activities from both categories at the same time throughout the school year.

Get to Know One Another

I have learned the importance of self-reflection and deeply looking into my own values and beliefs and unpacking my own history. Without doing so I do not believe it is possible to move forward with the work nor be able to think about how we might engage children in thinking and talking about diversity.

—Teacher

One of the central themes of anti-bias education is educators knowing who they are and sharing their identities and life experiences with each other. This ongoing interchange deepens collegial relationships and sets the precedence for learning about families and children. You can use the following getting-to-know-each-other activities at staff retreats or staff meetings at the beginning of and throughout the school year.

Potato Activity. This is an icebreaker, intended for staff for whom talking about diversity is relatively new or uncomfortable. The purpose is twofold. One is to get participants talking about differences—in this case, the many ways a potato is a potato. The second is to introduce the idea that learning opportunities for exploring diversity exist in daily early childhood activities and materials. To implement the potato activity:

1. Put enough potatoes on a central table so there is at least one per person.
2. Ask participants to describe what they see as the characteristics of potatoes; write their responses on a large sheet of paper.
3. Invite each person to choose one potato and study it closely for 5 minutes.
4. Collect the potatoes, and put them back in a large box.
5. Ask all participants to find their potato. Then ask, "How did you identify your potato?" Record answers next to the first list.
6. Ask the whole group to consider differences and similarities in the two lists. Typically words in the first list are general and objective (e.g., *brown, lumpy, oval, different sizes, roundish*), while phrases in the second list are individualized and suggestive of a specific potato (e.g., *has a frown, two dots, fits in the palm of my hand*).
7. Engage participants in reflecting on the activity. Use questions such as, "What did you do to get to know your potato well?" "What did you learn from this activity?" "How can you apply these lessons to people?"

As the program leader, you should facilitate the brainstorming, adding your own reflections, which are the central ideas you want participants to consider:

- There are many different ways to think about people (as there are with potatoes), once you get to know them.
- As with potatoes, people are complex, made up of many characteristics and identities.
- A potato, like a person, is both a member of a larger group and a particular individual.

Cultural-Identity Narratives. Story telling with staff about who they are rests on the premise that they all grew up and now live within a cultural framework that affects relationships with each other as well as their work with children and families. This activity makes these influences visible by naming and exploring participants' backgrounds.

Some people find it difficult to publicly share their stories, so it is important to acknowledge the risk taking. You should break the ice by telling your cultural story first. Providing structure to the activity with clear goals and outcomes also provides safety. There are no "right" questions to open up cultural storytelling about oneself. They should come from reading your group and beginning with questions that make sense to the group. As staff get to know

each other, then you can scaffold questions that deepen the conversations.
Topics that stimulate stories about family culture include telling about:

- A meaningful family cultural artifact and why it is significant
- The reasons for one's first and family names
- A favorite ritual or holiday and what was important about it
- How an individual's family came to live in the United States

You should facilitate the storytelling, inviting individuals to clarify and expand their stories, and engaging the group in reflecting on the similarities, differences, and themes that emerge from the stories.

Culture in Your Bag. This activity can be done on the spot as an icebreaker with no preparation. It reflects the concept that we carry our culture with us all the time. In this activity everyone has a partner. In pairs, the participants share what is in their bag (pocket or wallet) and what these objects reveal (either literally or metaphorically) about their identity and culture. For example, one teacher pulled out a set of keys and said it reminded her of her parents being immigrants and entering this country. After the participants have a chance to share in pairs, then they can share in the large group. To encourage relationship building and active listening, the partners in each pair introduce each other to the large group by relating the partner's story in brief.

A variation of this activity is to have each person create a cultural bag as a homework assignment. The participants put five things in a brown paper bag that represent who they are and their culture. Then they share their bags at a staff meeting in one of several ways; for example,

- Each participant can share his or her bag and explain the significance of each item.
- The anonymous bags can be arranged on a table. Each person picks a bag, looks at the objects, and then tries to guess who it belongs to and why.

In all of these variations the main purpose of the activity is to have participants gain a better understanding of what is meant by culture and from this perspective to get to know each other. Sharing a brief text like "Culture: A Process That Empowers" (Phillips, 1995), which succinctly clarifies the core ideas, can help teachers understand the concepts better.

Uncovering Attitudes We Were Taught. Asking staff to identify and examine their attitudes about different kinds of identity diversity is also key to their growth in anti-bias work. At the beginning of this activity, it helps participants' sense of safety if you say a few words about how we all learn negative attitudes as we grow up. As with other activities, you can model being open about this topic. Responding to the following questions from *Anti-Bias Education for Young Children and Ourselves* (Derman-Sparks & Edwards, 2010) provides places to start:

- What memories do you have of what your family or other caregivers taught you about various kinds of diversity among people? Was their behavior consistent with what they said?
- What do you remember from childhood about how you made sense out of human differences? What confused you?
- What did you learn in school about whom you should and shouldn't be friends with? What were you taught about how and why people were different? Were the same messages taught at home?
- What childhood experiences did you have with peers or adults who were different from you in some way (racial identity, culture/ethnicity, family structure, economic class, religion, gender role, sexual orientation)? Were these experiences comfortable? Why or why not?
- As an adult, in what ways do you agree or disagree with your parents'/guardian's views about the various groups. If you disagree, how did you develop your own, different ideas? (p. 23)

Diversity Rounds. The objectives of this activity are to become more aware of one's multiple identities, to work with others to define identities, and to think more deeply about what diversity means. Leading this large group activity, you ask participants to group and regroup themselves in four or five different ways. Based on the prompt the leader calls out, participants talk with each other to define and form their own categories. Sample prompts may be:

- Where were you born?
- What is your birth order?
- What kind of school did you attend growing up?
- When you think of your identity what comes to mind first?

As each group forms, participants discuss:

1. What does it mean to you to be (a member of this group)?
2. How important is this group to how you define yourself?
3. How is our group unique?

This protocol was created by educators and affiliates with the School Reform Initiative (2014a). Complete directions for this activity are available at the SRI website (www.schoolreforminitiative.org).

Identity Webs. The identity web is one effective way to begin exploring social identities. It rests on the premise that everyone has many personal and social identities. The idea of "social identities" may be new for many staff. (Refer to Chapter 1 for a full explanation of social identities.) In this activity each staff member is given a blank identity web. The web is a circle with spokes generating from the center (it looks like a drawing of a sun).

Ask participants to write their name in the middle of the web. On each spoke they should write their identities (e.g., "Asian" or "male" or "Jewish"), or the qualities (e.g., intelligent, compassionate, strong) they believe make them who they are. Participants list as many or as few aspects of their identity and qualities as they wish. After staff members complete their individual webs, they share them in pairs, along with something they learned about themselves by doing this activity. Then you should facilitate a large-group discussion about the whole activity.

In addition to increasing participants' understanding about themselves, the identity web activity opens up issues about the differences between personal and social identities and which aspects of their social identities they are comfortable revealing, which are more difficult to reveal, and the sources of their discomfort and comfort. Some individuals want to shift to the comfort of individual identities and differences as a way to avoid talking about social categories. For example, some staff members might not want to initially disclose their sexual orientation, social class, or religion until they feel more comfortable with the group. These discoveries lead staff to examine more deeply the impact of individual and societal prejudice and discrimination.

The final part of the Identity Web activity is to investigate how our identities influence our roles as educators and parents. Below are some responses to this question from teachers:

- Being a White female makes me even more interested in learning about other cultures and more aware of how much I don't know.
- Being a child of an immigrant family, I have learned the value of cultural differences.
- Having experienced being an insider and outsider in various groups throughout my life has influenced my belief that inaccuracy and imbalance diminish all of us.

To deepen staff's understanding of social identities, you can use the following questions from *Anti-Bias Education for Young Children and Ourselves* (Derman-Sparks & Edwards, 2010) to open up further conversations. Invite staff to first think about the questions, share their responses in dyads, and then discuss specific questions with the whole group.

- Make a list of all the various social identities you have now (e.g., related to your appearance, work, economic status, family statuses). Which social identities have brought you rewards? Which ones brought you prejudice and discrimination or limited your access to social institutions? Which have been more difficult for you?

- What did your family teach you about your various social identities? What messages were overt, and which covert?
- How did schools help or hurt you in your various social identities? Did you feel that you and your family were visible or invisible in the learning materials and curriculum?
- What overt and covert lessons might young children get from their favorite TV programs? Who is visible? Who is invisible? About which groups are there positive or negative messages? (p. 14)

COMMITTING TO AN ANTI-BIAS EDUCATION FRAMEWORK

I used to think that showing my anti-bias attitude meant not highlighting or bringing up differences, but I have learned that discussing and celebrating these differences in a more active way is a very powerful tool against bias.

—Teacher

In the first months of a program year the leader should provide regular opportunities for the staff to advance their grasp of the core concepts of anti-bias education.

Introduce Anti-Bias Education

Workshops and staff meetings that introduce and review the purpose, values, and goals of anti-bias education reflect the program leader's commitment. Learning activities about anti-bias education begin at staff orientation and the first staff meeting of the year and continue regularly as an incremental series of experiences.

As program leaders and teacher educators, Debbie and John did several introductory sessions with staff and their students. They included an exploration of the rationale for anti-bias education, a discussion on how ABE differs from other approaches to diversity, and a self-reflection activity that focuses on the meaning of anti-bias education for each person.

Noticing Differences. Ask staff to think back to their work with children or their own childhood experience for examples in which a child/children noticed another child or adult who was different from them in one or more of the following ways: disability, race (skin color), language, gender, sexual orientation/family composition, religion, or ethnicity. What are the comments or questions that are voiced when they notice the difference? The goal is to have participants think about the wide range of differences and the different ages when children notice differences. After staff have had time to think and write silently, they share their comments in pairs, small groups, and the whole group. As the facilitator, you write the comments and child's age on chart paper (e.g., 4-year-old: Why does he talk funny? 3-year-old: Why is her skin dirty? 5-year-old: Look at that person in the wheel chair). You then ask the participants to discuss how adults respond when they hear these comments and questions from children. Examples of responses have included:

- Ignore the comment
- Reflect the question back to the child
- Get more information from the child
- Answer the child very matter-of-factly
- Correct the child with adult's desired response

In processing this activity the main point is for staff to understand that while children are aware of differences at very young ages, how adults respond to the children's responses make a huge difference. The adult response can reinforce that it is not good to ask questions about differences or that it is okay to notice differences and it is okay to be different. As a follow-up, you could provide a handout on children's developmental stages of awareness of differences (York, 2003).

Diversity Education Continuum. The purpose of this activity is for participants to articulate the differences between anti-bias education and other approaches to diversity. As the facilitator your job is to provide a framework for the staff to think about the different approaches to diversity in schools. On a piece of chart paper, you can draw a big line with two arrows at each end to show this is a continuum. There are four terms on the line, from left to right:

Differences denial———Tourist curriculum———Nonbias——Anti-Bias

You should explain that this continuum represents different ways to think and teach about differences. Give the participants a definition for each term, and then ask participants to relate their school experiences to the four terms on the continuum by providing examples and additional descriptors. You can write their ideas on the chart paper in columns under each term. As in previous activities, you facilitate the activity by providing the core ideas you want the staff to understand:

- In a *differences-denial* approach, the learning environment, curriculum, and teaching ignore and avoid diversity.
- In a *tourist* approach, differences are emphasized and often exaggerated. Children learn superficially about different cultures around the world, as a tourist would when visiting different places.

- A *nonbiased* approach focuses on creating an authentic, nonstereotypical classroom environment that acknowledges similarities and differences.
- An *anti-bias* perspective is an active and activist approach that respects each child's and family's background and reality, while introducing a working concept of diversity that directly addresses the impact of social stereotypes, bias, and discrimination in children's development and interactions.

Becoming an Anti-Bias Educator. Considering the meaning of anti-bias education for themselves and their work is another important beginning-of-year discussion for staff, as it also becomes a way to check changes in thinking as the school year progresses. You should introduce (or review) the four core goals of anti-bias education listed in Chapter 1. Then ask staff to think about relevant questions, such as the following from *Anti-Bias Education for Young Children and Ourselves* (Derman-Sparks & Edwards, 2010), and to share their responses with their colleagues:

- What do the anti-bias goals mean to you?
- What do you hope anti-bias education will do for the children you teach? If your hopes are realized, how will it benefit them?
- What do you hope anti-bias education will do for their families? How will it benefit them?
- What anxieties and concerns do you have about doing anti-bias education in your setting?
- Where will you find support for doing anti-bias education within or outside your program? (p. 20)

You should also enter into the staff's discussion of these questions. Having them see you as a learner who is willing to be open and vulnerable about where you are on the anti-bias journey allows them to take more risks.

Articulate an Anti-Bias Mission Statement

Even though anti-bias education has always been part of the mission of this school, our level of engagement shifted when we began to have more focused conversations about it.

—Teacher

Every anti-bias program needs an articulated anti-bias statement about its mission, goals, and values. This statement can be a separate mission statement, or it can be embedded in the program philosophy or core values of the program. These statements become a part of the program's policies and are visible in the program's staff and family handbooks.

An anti-bias mission statement is the operational framework that lays down what a program will do about anti-bias education. It is a foundational building block, giving direction and accountability markers to what the leader and staff hope to accomplish. As program leader, you should have a clear sense of what an anti-bias vision and mission encompass from the start, but it can't be just one person's idea. Establishing a mission that actually becomes part of a program's ongoing organizational structure, culture, policies, procedures, and daily practices demands collaborative participation of the educators. Take some time to do this, but do not let the process get bogged down, so that it becomes a way to avoid actually making anti-bias changes. Once your program has agreed on a diversity/anti-bias mission statement, it then becomes a framework for taking stock of where you are, what you have done, and where you want to go next.

When a program has an established anti-bias mission statement, it is not necessary to reconstruct a new one every year. However, you do need to reestablish staff understanding and sense of ownership of the mission each year.

The Program's First Anti-Bias Mission Statement. Asking staff to state their ideas about "What would your center look like if it were an excellent anti-bias program?" is a valuable beginning step for developing your program's mission statement. Next, it is useful to involve staff in considering what bearing NAEYC's (2011) *Code of Ethical Conduct and Statement of Commitment*, and the general philosophy of your program, have on an anti-bias mission.

If your staff is small, it is possible to draft your mission statement together. You can write a first draft, based on the staff's thoughts in the discussion previously described, and invite their feedback. In the case of a large staff, drafting a mission statement all together becomes cumbersome. Establishing a staff leadership task force is one effective way to begin the mission statement process. Start with staff whom you have identified as sharing an anti-bias perspective, who have done some type of diversity work in their classrooms, or who have explored their own issues of identity. In John's first year as director at the CSDC he formed the Diversity, Equity, and Bias Taskforce (DEBT) with five interested teachers, as he describes below:

Together we drafted a diversity mission statement, which incorporated the staff's vision of an anti-bias program [see Figure 4.1]. I provided examples from other schools and the anti-bias education goals to help us get started. While I was concerned that this could be a distraction from action, it was vital to name the center's vision of anti-bias education work and have a public document that set a basis for accountability.

Broader language from the university's diversity statement was intentionally included in our mission as a way to ally the center with the larger institution. This language is helpful in being explicit about the range of human diversity. We were also careful in using words like *strive* to indicate that the program was not there yet, but making a concerted effort.

The task force distributed the draft mission statement to all staff for feedback, discussion, and reaching consensus about the final version. We made it available to

Figure 4.1. Example of a Program's Diversity/Anti-Bias Mission Statement

Diversity/Anti-Bias Mission Statement

We believe that human diversity is integral to the care and education of young children and to all those who touch their lives. Diversity in our community means a fully inclusive campus community that is enriched by persons of different races, genders, ethnicities, nationalities, economic backgrounds, ages, abilities, sexual orientation and gender identity or expression, and religious beliefs. Our goal is to promote awareness and acceptance, affirm equity, and take an active stance against bias in our community.

We strive to respect and value the differences in each child and family in our community through all that we do. We value the development of strong relationships with families and colleagues in order to better understand how we can respond to cultural and historical differences in experiences, values, and practices. We offer an environment that welcomes and celebrates the sharing of family history and culture in the classroom in meaningful ways. In our curriculum we are intentional in providing children with opportunities to explore similarities and variation, and we are responsive to the questions that emerge.

We support children in being active participants in their world by connecting them to their community in ways that foster an understanding of diversity and an ability to effect change. We are committed to an open and ongoing dialogue among colleagues, families, and the students we mentor, seeking insight into how we contribute to social bias and the process of change. As adults we strive to be models of active participation in our field by speaking out against bias and seeking equity.

Note. Adapted from "Diversity Commitment," by Child Study and Development Center, 2005.

families, in handouts, on the bulletin board, and on our website, thus making public the center's desire to honor diversity. Two important outcomes occurred: We began connecting with families who fully supported the diversity work, and families began to explicitly hold us accountable to the mission statement. Each year we read the mission statement in training to keep it alive.

When an Anti-Bias Mission Statement Exists. Attaining staff engagement with the anti-bias mission when it has already become part of the program's culture calls for other strategies, as Debbie explains:

At the Eliot–Pearson Children's School, anti-bias education has been part of the policy handbooks for many years. It is fully integrated into the core philosophy and framework goals for the school. However, the community reviews the core values underlying the statement each year at an early staff meeting and also at an early meeting of families. The objective is for the community to understand and feel involved with the mission statement. When I was the program leader, we read and examined the mission statement and core frameworks together in small groups using the Four "A"s Text Protocol [for the full protocol, see School Reform Initiative, 2014b.] Then the whole group discussed the following prompts:

- What *assumptions* does the text (diversity statement) hold?
- What do you *agree* with in the text?
- What do you want to *argue* with in the text?
- What parts of the text do you want to *aspire* to (or *act* upon)?

While changes to the underlying values of program's existing anti-bias values and mission statement usually weren't made, we did use this process to modify sections that we felt did not fully capture core values or needed clarification.

Set Anti-Bias Goals

It's a kind of trickle-down anti-bias approach. The director has an anti-bias education agenda for the school, but at the same time, allows teachers to have their own agendas for the classrooms. The teachers allow their teaching assistants to have their agendas. Everyone is coming from a different place with different questions, and interests, and the director brings it all together under this big umbrella.

—Teacher

Once the program has an anti-bias mission statement, the next step is to set concrete implementation goals for making the anti-bias approach come alive. You will need to consider three types of goals that are typical of high-quality programs: program-wide goals, classroom team goals, and individual staff goals.

Program-wide Goals. These are goals that affect the entire program and draw on the contributions of all the staff and potentially families. Examples of goals that explicitly seek to implement your anti-bias approach include updating the program's collection of diversity and anti-bias books, expanding family education opportunities, and offering teachers professional development on specific anti-bias topics. While program anti-bias goal setting needs to be a collaborative process, the program leader sets the expectation for implementing these goals, making clear that all educators need to engage in the anti-bias commitment. John offers an illustration of this:

When I began my work at CSDC, the teachers' proposals for goals that we could work on together did not include any reference to diversity. I decided to add an explicit, but broad, anti-bias goal to the list and connect this to the teachers' espoused humanist values of care, community, and respect. I felt it was important to create an initial starting place for our anti-bias efforts.

Another time for the program leader to take the lead in revisiting and setting program-wide goals is when anti-bias efforts lag or stagnate.

Classroom Team Goals. Teaching teams set the goals for their specific classroom's work, within the framework of the school goals. Examples of classroom goals include enhancing the types of props the teaching team puts in the dramatic play center to make it more culturally relevant to the population they serve, introducing the use of storytelling to facilitate discussions with children about differences and bias, observing the children's thinking about gender, and developing activities to scaffold learning experiences about gender. After the teachers identify their classroom goals, they share them in writing with the program leader, who coaches teaching teams through supervision on how they plan to work on their goals and help them revisit the goals periodically throughout the year.

Individual Teacher Goals. This level of goal setting includes each teacher's personal growth, practice with children, and relationships with the families of the children in the class. The framework of the anti-bias mission statement, as well as the program-wide and classroom team goals, set an initial direction. Individual goal setting enables teachers to begin each year at their own level of anti-bias education ability. These initial individual goals also give the program leader information about where each teacher is on the anti-bias journey.

In Figure 4.2 is a sample of individual teacher beginning goals and more advanced goals. Teachers specify what they will work on, how they will do it, and what kinds of support they need from the program leader.

Develop a Critical Eye About the Learning Environment

Providing a physical learning environment that is free of misinformation and stereotypes and rich in diversity is another major component of shifting the culture of a program. It is essential to incorporate changes in the physical learning environment to reflect the program's anti-bias mission statement, goals, and professional development. As program leader, you should facilitate educators developing a critical eye about the materials they provide to the children. Several excellent resources offer tools for building anti-bias material learning environments (see online resources in Appendix A at www.tcpress.com).

Book Survey. This is an example of one specific activity for cultivating a critical anti-bias education eye. Teachers and other staff educators work together to review all the children's books in the program. To get on the same page about the issues to consider, they first read a checklist tool, such as the one

Figure 4.2. Individual Teacher Goals

Anti-Bias Goal	What I Will Do	Support I Need from My Supervisor
BEGINNING TEACHER GOALS		
Become more comfortable responding to children's comments and questions about differences.	Respond to their questions; keep track of the comments and questions.	Give me suggestions on how to respond.
Read more books on same-sex families to the class.	Research what books are available and appropriate for my age group.	Find funds for me to purchase the books. Give me suggestions on how to introduce a book. What should I tell families?
MORE ADVANCED TEACHER GOALS		
Write a persona doll script about a child who is homeless.	Read and research more about the issues for a child who is homeless.	Help me find appropriate resources; meet with me to review the script.
Document my skin color curriculum.	Keep notes; find time to write them up. Prepare a conference presentation.	Give me some structure to keep me accountable; find funds for me to attend a conference.

on the Teaching for Change website (Derman-Sparks, 2013b). After reviewing the books, the teachers and other staff educators discuss which books they want to continue to use and what to do with books containing misinformation and stereotypical images and/or messages of particular groups. For example, some books may not be appropriate for young preschoolers, but useful to open up conversation with older children about why a book may be "unfair." They also identify what people and ways of life are missing in their collection and prioritize purchasing new books.

Scavenger Hunt. This activity introduces the topic of the learning environment. The program leader creates a list of classroom materials that could be used for anti-bias education in the program. The educators divide into several teams, and each group looks for the items on their list. The lists may be different items, or they can be a category of similar items. Examples of items that could be included are the following:

- A book about two moms or two dads
- Art materials to make self-portraits reflecting all the children and staff
- Posters showing girls and boys doing a range of activities
- Play food reflective of all children
- Charts (numbers, colors, songs) labeled in different languages
- Dolls with different skin tones

When the scavenger hunt is over, participants gather the materials they have found in the school and then discuss how they could use these materials with children for anti-bias education. During the discussion and analysis, the program leader may find that some materials found by the teachers are problematic or incomplete in some way. For example a teacher may bring a poster of two Asian children but with very stereotypic clothing or gender roles. The leader and teacher discuss how they could use this poster with the children, "When would these children wear the kimono? Is it for a special occasion?" The teachers could also discuss how to adapt readily available early childhood materials to explore anti-bias concepts, such as adding photos of children of different racial or ethnic backgrounds to the unit blocks.

Once educators have assessed their anti-bias teaching materials, and identified what they still need (or need to dispose of), you should look at ways to allocate funds or figure out other ways to acquire the materials. For instance, by building relationships with businesses in the community, you may be able to obtain donations of materials or funds to support workshops with families and staff to make materials. Engaging staff members in researching and making decisions about new purchases *and* thinking creatively about how to best use limited resources is in itself a useful anti-bias professional development experience.

BEING A LIFE-LONG LEARNER

It takes a lot of work, but there are many ways to engage in anti-bias work that promote positive and challenging discussion and help educators view themselves as advocates for fairness and equity. As the program leader, your charge is to lead the way, keep the mission and expectations clear, and bring the staff along. This does not mean that you need to know all the answers. By modeling being a learner, taking risks, and working collaboratively with staff to figure it all out step by step, you can live the anti-bias approach.

In Chapter 6 we return to a focus on teachers and their professional development, but in the next chapter we turn to strategies for program leaders in working with families. As with the staff, program leaders have a vital role in ensuring that families are aware of, come to appreciate, and support anti-bias education.

CHAPTER 5

Engaging Families and Growing Anti-Bias Partnerships

Families do and don't feel like they fit in for a whole range of reasons. We want to be heard, valued, and included in ways that seem meaningful and valuable to us.

—Parent

The participation of families is fundamental to building a meaningful anti-bias education program. The program leader is responsible for fostering family belonging, trust, and engagement, as well as promoting strong teacher–family relationships. As leader, you make sure that the program's anti-bias values and goals are transparent to the community, put into practice a range of strategies for family involvement, and facilitate problem solving when there is a disagreement over anti-bias issues.

In this chapter we begin with a discussion about levels of family engagement within anti-bias education. We then describe a variety of strategies for working with families.

THE FRAMEWORK FOR WORKING WITH FAMILIES

I have a better understanding of what building meaningful relationships, trust, care, and respect involves as we learn about each individual family and are responsive to the diversity they bring to the classrooms.

—Teacher

The foundation for working with families begins with a willingness to engage in reciprocal partnerships, to exchange information and learn from them, and to provide a welcoming stance for all families. Families must first feel accepted, respected, and part of the program's community in order to engage actively with anti-bias issues. Having an inclusive definition of families is essential.

An Inclusive View of Families

Families come in different constellations, including single-parent families, same-sex families, extended families, blended families, two-parent working families, foster families, and adoptive families. These differences can mean that families vary in their relationship to and experience of specific anti-bias issues. Families also belong to various subgroups (e.g., racial, ethnic, socioeconomic class), which affects their everyday lives. In a program with an anti-bias approach, families should be able to answer yes to the question, "Do I see who I am, who my child is, who my family is in the program's environment and curriculum?" Essential, too, is a program culture where members seek to acknowledge, share, and nurture diversity in the community.

Home–program partnerships are a two-way street, built on mutual trust (Allen, 2007; Berger, 2008; Gonzalez-Mena, 2012). In anti-bias family partnerships, early childhood programs see families as reservoirs of knowledge and expertise, central to understanding the children they serve (Gonzalez, Moll, & Amanti, 2005). While both home and program need to be open to learning from each other, the program sets the tone for dialogue and learning. Program leaders and teachers also must feel comfortable sharing power with families.

Learning about families is a process, not a one-time event. It begins at the start of the year and then continues as families develop more familiarity, comfort, and trust with the teachers and program leader. Families differ in when and how much they choose to disclose about their lives. Program leaders, as well as teachers, should take this into account in how they learn about the families they serve. As teachers' skill in building relationships with families grows, they feel more confident about how to raise sensitive topics (Park, Lee-Keenan, & Given, in press).

Building an effective anti-bias family partnership incorporates best ECCE practices with families. Programs need to provide multiple ways for families to interface with the program since families differ in their life experiences, expectations of school, and how they raise children. Program leaders should value the contributions all families make, from getting their child to school prepared for the day, to being on a family advisory board. Participation should be made as accessible as possible by having events at different times and providing child care and food. Leaders should not expect families to take part in everything, but should try to offer some opportunities that mesh with their skills, energy, and availability.

Levels of Family Engagement with Anti-Bias Work

Everyone in the community is at their own comfort level with anti-bias education and different topics.

—Parent

Families come to a program with varying levels of commitment to the community and its mission. Some families may have explicitly chosen a program based on the anti-bias mission, while others may be there due to reputation, convenience, or other more pragmatic considerations. They are beginning their own anti-bias journeys from different starting points. For many, anti-bias education is a new concept and educational approach. Even families that chose the program because of its commitment to ABE might find that actually participating in the community is asking more of them than they had expected. Coming to understand what the goals of ABE are, how young children develop their identity and attitudes, and how ABE infuses all aspects of a program takes time and effort. In addition, various issues going on in families' lives may affect their responses to an anti-bias approach. As the program leader, it is your responsibility, in conjunction with the teachers, to identify where a family is in relation to anti-bias work, and to know where to start in order to support their understanding and engagement.

One frequent question about involving families in ABE is how to do this without making them uncomfortable. Opening up issues of identity and bias is inevitably uncomfortable at times. This is because prejudice and discrimination hurt individuals—directly when they are the targets and indirectly when they face how they may have participated in hurtful behavior. It is also because most people at a young age learned to be silent about prejudice and discrimination. Either it isn't considered a polite topic, or for targets it is dangerous to talk openly about the effects of discrimination.

Therefore, the more useful question is, "How do we create a supportive place for people to begin or continue engaging with anti-bias education from wherever they are?" This requires building a community where all members feel that they are seen and heard, and that they belong. It also means taking into account and respecting at all times each person's place on the anti-bias engagement progression.

Over the years, Debbie and John identified a progression for family engagement in anti-bias activities that unfolds over time. Family members enter at different levels and move through the progression with varying speed and duration. This progression can be a useful guide for you in choosing relevant family-engagement strategies.

1. Families first learn about the anti-bias commitment and mission of program. This happens during preadmission tours and orientation meetings with the program leader, and by reading the family handbook and mission statements. Depending on the visibility of your anti-bias efforts outside of the program, families may enter at Levels 2 or 3 below.
2. Families begin to understand what being part of an anti-bias community means through family education opportunities about specific anti-bias topics.
3. Families begin to participate in classroom activities and initiate conversations with teachers or the program leader about anti-bias education. They may share family cultural practices in their child's classroom (e.g., send

family artifacts, record a story in their home language, or demonstrate a holiday ritual), help create anti-bias learning materials, and work with staff to resolve disagreements regarding anti-bias issues and teaching practices counter to their cultural beliefs.

4. Families become allies of anti-bias efforts. They advocate anti-bias values and actively engage with other families and the staff in related issues and activities. They may participate in family and family–teacher discussion groups, communicate their ideas about anti-bias work to the staff, and provide input to the anti-bias program.

5. Families provide leadership. They take the lead in initiating new anti-bias strategies and related activities, participate in making decisions about the program, and actively bring their anti-bias perspective to various program groups (e.g., coleader of diversity group, program advisory group, or teacher search committee).

The year will typically begin with families reflecting a range of anti-bias levels. Many will be at Level 1 or 2, and some are at Level 3. However, in programs that form with an explicit anti-bias mission, many families may be ready to engage with anti-bias work at Levels 3, 4, and 5. As the year progresses, most families advance their understanding and involvement. While the proportion of families at the leadership level is usually small, they play an indispensable role in shifting the program to an anti-bias culture. Later in this chapter we discuss strategies designed to engage families at various points in their participation.

INTRODUCING ANTI-BIAS VALUES AND EXPECTATIONS

I learned that anti-bias is very broad and not limited to race, culture, and ethnicity, and it's a lot more than just celebrating different holidays.

—Parent

Families begin learning about a program's anti-bias mission even before the school year begins. This education begins in orientation and intake, and then continues during the year, as families build familiarity and trust with the teachers and the program leader.

Preadmission

Programs have opportunities to reach out, educate, and inform potential families about anti-bias education before enrolling their children. This outreach may be part of efforts to diversify the demographics of your program, sometimes in response to government regulations. In addition to having explicit language about your anti-bias approach in application and promotional materials, we have found it is important to be intentional about including anti-bias education language as a priority in any tour of the program that families attend.

Intake and Orientation Process

The intake process is an opportunity for families to begin to share information about themselves and their home culture. You should make sure that the wording and questions of application and admissions paperwork reflect respect for diversity and acknowledges that the child's primary caretakers may be other than a mother or father (e.g., using "guardian one" and "guardian two"). The intake questionnaire should include specific questions about languages spoken at home, important traditions, cultural beliefs about childrearing and education, and how families identify their race, ethnicity, religion, and family structure.

Family Goal Form. Completing this form early in the school year enables families to describe their child's unique characteristics, interests, likes and dislikes, strengths and challenges, as well as list their hopes and expectations for their child. You should make it possible for families to answer the family goal form either orally or in writing, and provide translation as necessary to help ensure that all families feel welcome in the community. Reviewing families' responses provides important learning for you and the teachers.

Program Open House. By inviting families to visit the program before a child attends, you offer an informal opportunity for families to see the classrooms and chat with you and the teachers. An alternative would be to structure a few days of transition for new families in which parents engage in observation and conversation at the program while the child attends.

A gathering at a local playground or park at the start of the year offers families a chance to begin to connect with one another and for staff to begin to learn about families through informal conversations. Debbie offers the following examples:

We first learned that a dad was in a wheel chair at a summer picnic and were able to be proactive about preparing the program for his visit. In another situation we discovered at an open house that a grandmother was the primary caregiver for one of the children enrolling.

Family Handbook and Program Website. Anti-bias goals, values, and relevant policies should be visible in your program's family handbook and website. Being clear about the program's goals for staff–family relationships is another proactive strategy for ensuring that conflicts result in meaningful solutions and growth. John explains how staff–family relations were developed at CSDC:

The staff generated the following goals as part of defining an anti-bias partnership with families:

- Ensure families feel welcomed and included as valued members of the center community
- Commit to the inclusion of different perspectives and searching for common ground
- Pay attention to the needs of the entire community, rather than just individuals

Parents on the advisory committee reviewed the goals and considered, "Can we hold the program accountable to work on meeting these goals?" Once staff and families agreed, the goals became part of the policy handbook. When new families came for an admissions tour, they received a handout that included these goals for developing a partnership with families.

I also developed a policy for adult conduct as a proactive strategy to help create a safe place for discussion and conflict [see Figure 5.1 for an excerpt]. Teachers found the language helpful because it provided clarity about the difference between conflict and disrespectful behavior.

Frequently Asked Questions. Even when families know that anti-bias education is a core value in the program, they have questions. Once a family starts attending, the reality is often different from what a family expected. Families who are part of privileged social-identity groups (e.g., White, heterosexual) may have a hard time understanding the benefits of anti-bias education for their children. They might equate the inclusion of other cultural and social perspectives in the curriculum as a loss for them and question where they fit in. Others may really believe that their culture is the superior and only "right" way to live. Some may also worry that by embracing anti-bias values they

Figure 5.1. Example of an Adult-Conduct Policy

Conduct of Adult Community Members Policy

As members of a community, adults at the center should strive to provide the children with a model of civil and respectful behavior. Interactions between adults should support a caring and safe environment for everyone.

Given that differences in opinions can arise, it is important that adults are aware of the behavior children observe when there is the potential for conflict. Children can learn a great deal by seeing adults approach and solve differences in a positive way.

Regardless of the problem, we expect community members to approach differences in opinion with an open mind and with respect for the other person and program policies. Language or behavior that is disrespectful, discriminatory, or abusive to others, including children, is never acceptable at the center.

Note. Adapted from *Family Handbook*, by Child Study and Development Center, 2011, p. 31.

will come into conflict with other members of the dominant group, including members of their own extended family.

Families from socially marginalized groups (e.g., people with disabilities, People of Color) may also express resistance to aspects of anti-bias education (Derman-Sparks, 2011). They may not trust how others will teach their children about identity or want to protect their children as long as possible from the hurt of knowing about prejudice. They may hold prejudices toward an aspect of social identity or have internalized negative ideas about their own groups. Some families whose first language is not English may object to early childhood programs cultivating both home language and English because they worry their children will not learn English sufficiently to progress successfully in school. They may not be aware of research demonstrating the limitations of an English-only approach in mastering a second language, as well as the harm of losing the home language at an early age (Garcia, 2010).

Over the years, we have found that certain questions about anti-bias education always come up. Debbie explains how responding to these questions was handled at the EPCS:

We created a Frequently Asked Questions (FAQ) handout for families, involving teachers and families in its development. We felt that putting the FAQ document in the family handbook and on our website would provide answers to some common questions, jumpstart families asking others, and provoke discussion. We began writing the FAQ with questions from our fall family curriculum night and our annual parent survey, which asks, "*What do you want to know about anti-bias education?*" Some of their questions included:

- What do children learn in an ABE environment?
- What is the role of families in anti-bias education?
- How does anti-bias education relate to bullying?
- How do teachers decide what to teach? What types of similarities and differences are discussed with the children?
- How is anti-bias education integrated into the school day? What is the relationship between play, academics, and ABE?
- Is anti-bias education appropriate for young children? Will my child learn or acquire biases about others?
- How does the school discuss similarities and differences between families, in terms of their parenting styles, beliefs, and values?
- What do I do if I disagree with the school's anti-bias philosophy? Is there room for discussion when a family's approach is different from that of the school?
- How is anti-bias education related to special education inclusion?
- How are the teachers trained to use anti-bias education? How can teachers teach ABE in a responsive and sensitive way to children whose identities are different from their own?

The yearlong process of developing answers to these questions, served as one way to engage families in anti-bias work and build a teacher–family partnership, as well as creating a needed document for new families. Families engaged in dialogue about anti-bias issues and heard a range of views and beliefs. The process of sorting, examining, and responding to the questions at a staff meeting (*What were parents really asking by this question?*) was a professional development opportunity. We also invited families to attend a staff meeting to give feedback on a draft of the FAQ. I worked with a teacher and a parent to put the final draft together. As a result, everyone reached a deeper understanding of different perspectives, and new families had another entry point for their participation in ABE. [See Figure 5.2 for an example of the questions included in the EPCS Frequently Asked Questions Handout. The complete FAQ handout is available at ase.tufts.edu/epcs/aboutAnti-Bias.asp.]

Anti-Bias Education Newsletters. Periodic newsletters, emails, postings on a family bulletin board, and website stories are written forms of communication that offer opportunities for you and the teachers to build on and reinforce

Figure 5.2. Example of a Frequently Asked Questions Handout

What do children learn in an ABE environment?

Children learn about similarities and differences in people and communities. They are encouraged to act in ways that reflect anti-bias values and to stand up for things they feel are unfair. ABE is integrated into the classroom activities. It is both planned curriculum within the structure of the day, as well as natural "teachable moments" based on children's social interactions, conversations, and play. Anti-Bias curriculum topics come from the children, families, and teachers, as well as historical or current events. When children ask questions about differences, adults listen in order to facilitate conversations and responses.

How does ABE relate to bullying?

ABE is an example of an antibullying, prosocial curriculum because we are proactively teaching children how to fairly understand and respond when they encounter difference. Exploration of power and conflict are a natural part of this process. Creating and maintaining a classroom community where everyone feels safe and respected is an essential part of the teacher's role at every age level. During the first weeks of school, teachers develop "ground rules" or "classroom agreements" with the children. These may include words such as "We take care of each other. We don't use words or actions that hurt others." Teachers lead discussions and activities that foster understanding others' points of view and differences. Problem-solving strategies are directly taught.

Note. Adapted from "FAQs about Anti-Bias Education at the Eliot Pearson Children's School," by Eliot–Pearson Children's School (n.d.).

discussion about various anti-bias issues. You can share stories about what the children are doing related to anti-bias education and offer ideas for responding to their questions about their own and others' identities. You may also use these outlets to include short pieces about your thoughts, observations, and recommendations on current anti-bias issues such as offering perspectives on a holiday, like Columbus Day or Thanksgiving; connecting anti-bias education to current topics such as bullying and obesity; or expressing concerns about stereotyping in a new children's movie. In addition, these communications are an opportunity to model talking about aspects of social identity by sharing something significant about your own background and experiences in relation to anti-bias work.

Create Family Visibility and Connection

Not only is every child different, every family is different. From their culture, race, ethnicity, background, dynamic, home life, and beliefs, you can't assume two families from the same place will be the same.

—Parent

No matter how families come to a program, they have the right to feel visible and welcomed so that they can be full participants in creating the community. Program leaders and staff need to ask themselves the following questions:

- Do families feel included and welcomed?
- Do families feel they can share their opinions?
- Do families feel reflected in the program and welcomed to share who they are?

The practices and activities described below are intended to help you build inclusion of all families. Some activities are specifically for the beginning of the year, while you can implement others throughout the year to encourage family sharing.

Reaching Out. The leader's goal is to reach out actively to all families, being observant and conscious of who may not be feeling comfortable in the community. It is very important to be aware of your own comfort levels as you initiate interactions. Do you tend to gravitate to some families because you are more comfortable with them, while avoiding others? These preferences can reflect your social identity and experiences. Reaching out can happen informally throughout the day or during program-wide events, such as a school potluck dinner or class breakfast. Debbie describes ways she reached out to families at EPCS:

I tried to be in the front lobby during arrival and departure to greet families as they walked through the door. As a parent said to me, "I loved seeing the director every morning greeting my child and me when I walked in the door." We also hosted an informal midweek morning coffee in the entrance area to allow families to grab a cup of coffee or tea on their way to work if people had time. This was also another opportunity for me to check in with families briefly.

Family Walls. One place to set the anti-bias tone is in the entrance area of the program. Debbie talks about how this was done at EPCS:

We invited each person in the school (both children and staff) to provide a photo of their family to decorate a bulletin board in the entrance area. We explicitly defined family in a broad way and left the interpretation up to the family. It could be the people who live in your household, your extended family around the world, or you and your grandma. We also had a world map in the center of the bulletin board and invited people to put dots on the map, to show "which cultures are part of your family." We intentionally used "cultures" in the plural to acknowledge that more than one culture can make up a family. The bulletin board sparked conversation about both difference and similarity and acted as a focal point for everyone to connect.

You can also suggest that community members make drawings of their family or a collage of photos to represent their family. Individual classrooms can ask families to bring in photos to put in the children's cubby or on a classroom bulletin board or to make a class family book.

Welcome in Different Languages. Signs, resource materials, and books in languages spoken by the families in your program can make them feel at home. You could set up an adult space that includes literature, magazines, parenting books, and copies of the program newsletters in the home languages of your families. Translation services may be difficult or expensive for some programs, but even welcome signs in different languages on the program door or in the entrance make a difference. Asking families to help you with this task often makes them feel validated and empowered. If they cannot do the translation, they may be able to find a resource to help you with the task.

Family Artifact Bag. This activity is designed to encourage family sharing in the classroom. Each teacher obtains a cloth bag with a drawstring that is designated as a family artifact bag. Each child in a class takes home the family bag one time during the year. The family puts different family artifacts into the bag, and then the child and a family member come to school to share the items in their bag with the classroom. Photographs of each family and their artifacts from the bag can be used to make a scrapbook or bulletin board display for the entrance.

Family Boxes. In this activity each family decorates the inside of a shoebox to represent their family in any way they choose. Families use photos, words, drawings, paper collage, clay, and small toys to decorate their box. Materials should be made available for use at home, and families should be encouraged to use a variety of materials and interpretations. Families bring completed boxes to the program, and staff members join the boxes together with tape to make a family wall. Families are asked to explain their boxes to the children in the class, or the teachers can get the explanation by phone or email, or when families pick up their children. The wall of family boxes sparks conversations among families.

Family Book Bag. To carry out this activity, the staff first decides on a theme that will provoke anti-bias conversations, and then each classroom creates a book bag that includes a relevant children's book (appropriate to the developmental level of the class) and a journal. The book bag goes home each night with a different child. The family reads the book together and then draws a picture or writes about the book in the journal. Teachers can model the process first by responding in respectful and child-friendly ways. This will encourage families to read and respond to previous entries. Each semester the program chooses a different focus for the book topic such as families, ethnicity, ability, gender, or activism.

FAMILY ANTI-BIAS EDUCATION AND DIALOGUES: A TWO-WAY STREET

The climate of the school allows for dialogue and a safe place to exchange ideas.

—Parent

In creating opportunities for families to develop their understanding of anti-bias education, the program leader takes into account the various ways adults learn (e.g., small groups, hands-on activities, large group, and media), preferred communication styles, and where families are in their anti-bias journeys.

One example of an effective family anti-bias education approach was developed by Ellen Wolpert (1996), when she directed an all-day preschool located in a housing project in Boston. The following description of Ellen's program and approach to anti-bias education, along with the four example topics for family education meetings comes from her unpublished account of the program, written in 1996. The community preschool served families with low incomes, most of whom were People of Color, including a large number of recent immigrants from Haiti and Central America. Monthly staff–family gatherings of 2 hours or less were at the core of the program's work with families. Sessions were scheduled at the end of the preschool day, so families picking up their children could stay and participate. Dinner and child care were provided.

The staff–family gatherings enabled families to learn about the anti-bias curriculum approach and experience the anti-bias activities their children were doing as well as anti-bias staff development activities. The sessions also explored the ways people learn and are affected by bias; shared values, expectations, and strategies for dealing with bias with their children; and ways to challenge bias in themselves and in their environment. Ellen used staff planning for the discussion sessions as a time to develop anti-bias awareness and practice in staff.

Topics for the staff–family gatherings came from the following sources:

1. Areas of bias that staff and/or families identified as important to learn more about
2. Curriculum themes that were emerging from observations of the children in the classroom
3. Issues in the community or the media that were likely to affect the children

Ellen always introduced discussions about issues of bias by first having participants in pairs or small groups look back at their past and current experiences. Family discussion sessions repeated key themes and issues over the year to meet the needs of new families and to provide opportunities for people in the program to share their experiences and changes of perspective with newcomers.

Following are four examples of topic-focused discussion sessions that Ellen developed and implemented.

Identity and Memories of School

As a foundation for later discussions about anti-bias education, the purpose of this first staff–family gathering of the year was to facilitate people making connections between their own experiences and their hopes for their preschool children.

1. Introductions:
   a. In groups of three, each person talks about him- or herself for 2 minutes: name, relationship to school, anything you want to say about your family, where you are from, things you are particularly interested in or like to do, your ethnic background, anything else you would like to say about yourself.
   b. Each person introduces him- or herself to the whole group: name and one or two things you'd like the group to know about yourself.
2. Exploring school experiences:
   a. In small groups, each person talks about "What experiences in school made you feel good about what your family is like, ethnic and racial background, economic situation, physical differences, and being male

or female?" "What experiences in school made you feel not good about these parts of who you are?"

    b. In the whole-group discussion, each participant first shares thoughts from the small groups. Then everyone discusses, "What do you think teachers, school administrators, and other school staff could have done differently to better support positive feelings about who you are?"

        The resulting discussion tends to reveal the varying school experiences of adults in the community based on their social identity. In the process adults see both points of connection (familiarity) and differences (unfamiliarity), which challenge our assumptions. The discussion also provides an opportunity to begin to identify what families want for their children and what the educators want for children in their care.

Ethnicity and Language

        This discussion topic developed because children had been making comments about languages in their classrooms that reflected both curiosity and disrespect. For instance, children laughed and teasingly said, "You talk funny," when a child whose first language is Spanish pronounced "juice" as "yuice."

1. Discussion began in small groups about what experiences participants had (as a child/as an adult) in these situations:
    a. Learning a new language
    b. Not being understood
    c. Not understanding others
    d. Being uncomfortable with languages, dialects, and accents different from one's own
    e. Not respecting or being respected because of language or accent

Responses by family members were often very personal and included:

- Saying I speak French, rather than Creole, because of fear of being put down because I am Haitian
- Fear of losing the ability to speak with grandparents and other relatives as I learned English
- Fear of being talked about when I can't understand the language others are speaking

2. The whole group heard from small groups and then addressed these additional questions:

- How does this issue affect your children?
- What language experiences have they had?
- What have you, other children, or other adults done in response?
- What would you like to have done in your child's class related to this issue?

3. The program leader described what the center was doing about language issues, followed by families discussing these questions:

- What do you think about the suggestions for dealing with language issues?
- What ideas do you have?

The earlier discussions about prior experiences made a good bridge to the program leader's presentation of what the program was doing and wanted to do.

Unlearning Stereotypes About Indigenous Peoples

Children often see and absorb stereotypical images and information about Native Americans and other Indigenous Peoples from the media and society throughout the month of November. This staff–family gathering focused on what happens and how to challenge the misinformation.

1. The whole group brainstormed what they have learned about Native Americans (and/or other Indigenous Peoples from country of origin). As part of this process, the program leader displayed a collection of common stereotypes in cards, children's books, and clothing as a way to stimulate memories.
2. Small groups played a series of games with photo cards depicting contemporary Native Americans doing familiar activities (e.g., reading to children, playing football, cooking, and engaged in various occupations). Participants talked about what they think children learn from playing with these cards and then considered how the photos differed from what they had thought Native Americans looked like and what they did. They talked about the sources of any misinformation and stereotypes.
3. The small groups shared their findings regarding stereotypes and reality, along with ways to help children learn about all of our lives in school. Some participants expressed indignation that they had never learned the truth in school and that the media and peers continue to expose their older children to stereotypes and misinformation.

Community Activism

In a creative and fun way, this staff–family gathering addressed Goal 4 of the anti-bias education goals for children (see Chapter 1). In their classes the staff had read the children's book, *The Streets Are Free* (Kurusa, 2008), which is based on the true story of the children of the barrio of San Jose de la Urbina in Caracas, Venezuela. It tells what the children did when the mayor did not keep his promise to build a playground in their neighborhood. After hearing the story, the children turned Ellen's office into the office of the mayor and acted out the story. The staff decided to share with the families what the children were doing, as a positive way to discuss taking action in the face of unfairness.

1. Small groups of family and staff received copies of the book illustrations as a reporter's photos of an incident happening in the neighborhood of the story. Each group had the task of assigning captions to their photos.
2. The small groups then shared their captions with the whole group and discussion explored the different perspectives on the photos.
3. The program leader, role-playing a member of the neighborhood, told the group the story in the book from the neighbor's perspective.
4. The group then discussed the difference between their various perspectives of the story and those of the "people who live in the neighborhood," how people have different perspectives even when they see the same incident, and the importance of getting the perspective of the people involved in that situation.
5. This led to discussion of what actually happens in their own neighborhoods when "outsiders" repeat only the negative events and don't know the daily life of people in their communities.
6. The group discussed the activism in the story, and the program leader raised questions about involving the children in activism: How do the family members feel about the story? What do they think about the children going to the mayor? How do you feel about our reading stories that include protest and demonstration such as *The Streets Are Free*? Families' reaction indicated agreement with the idea of talking about activism with their children, as these two comments show:

> The story didn't go far enough! The community should have continued to demonstrate until the mayor did his job and built the playground.
>
>   My older daughter graduated from the preschool, and my younger daughter still goes here. Because of these kind of stories, when either one of them wants something but can't convince me, she gets the other to help get what she wants. My first reaction is to want to discipline them for arguing with me, but my second reaction is to figure ways to set good limits and also encourage them. I want them to stand up for things they believe in and to see how much better it is to work together. (Wolpert, 1996, p. 15)

PROMOTING FAMILY PARTNERSHIP AND LEADERSHIP

Beyond families engaging in education discussion and participating in activities for the children, an anti-bias approach requires building support and collaboration among families and leadership of families in the program's work. Here are some suggestions for ways to do this.

Family Support System

A community with an anti-bias focus provides ways for families to raise experiences with prejudice and discrimination either in the school or in the larger society. It then offers opportunities for families to support and be allies for each other. Depending on the specific situation, the program leader may offer support directly; sometimes the support comes from staff and other families. In addition, the program leader gathers a portfolio of support networks and resources as part of the reading of the program (see Chapter 3).

Being Available. As the program leader, you should be comfortably accessible to all families throughout the year. John and Debbie used the mantra, "My door is always open"—both figuratively and physically. They wanted families to feel safe to share concerns and discuss anti-bias issues as they arose. Debbie offers these comments:

My office was off the front entrance, and I tried to keep my door open (unless I was having a meeting), so families could pop in any time they wanted without a special appointment. Families often are more willing to share difficult issues with an open-door policy. Sometimes parents just need someone to listen, not talk. Ensuring that a parent feels heard, especially when sharing issues that are emotional, can go a long way in building trust. Other times, I needed to offer a resource, information, or a recommendation for further support, such as a social worker, adoption group, or other support group. Because anti-bias issues are complex, it is often helpful not to respond in depth at first and essentially say, "Let me think about that and get back to you." This provides you time to think through the issues, collect information, and consult others.

Resources Information. Some programs have a family resource area with books, pamphlets, and articles on a range of parenting issues. Access to websites and other electronic resources provides another useful source. Families might have access to the Internet at your program or be offered photocopied materials. In an anti-bias program the resource library includes specific materials on anti-bias topics that families can borrow to take home or read at the center. The program leader can research literature on issues such as families raising children adopted internationally, interracial families, children with cross-gender identity, or whatever specific concerns arise from the families in the program.

Diversity Dialogues Group. Functioning as a support and learning group, the Diversity Dialogue group at Eliot–Pearson Children's School meets monthly, co-led by a parent and staff person. Debbie notes:

The group defines *diversity* broadly, and anyone in the community may attend. At one point, some White families felt they were not welcome because they did not see themselves as "diverse." As the director, I used this situation as an opportunity to clarify that everyone has a culture and that together we create diversity. Diversity exists in the relationships between us, not in those who are different from us. The group also changed the name from "Diverse Families Group" to "Diversity Dialogues," which helped to alleviate the concerns of some White families that they would not be welcome.

Over the years topics for the meetings included adoption, multiracial families, religion, class, and handling bias when it occurs. Families often brought up dilemmas about identity or bias issues in their own and their children's lives, and asked for ideas about how to handle these situations. Sometimes the group read a specific article together or watched a video clip to jumpstart the conversation.

Depending on the family community and history of working on anti-bias education, you may find that in addition to diversity dialogue groups, support groups for a particular sociocultural group are needed. These "homogeneous" groups often help their members feel safer to open up about the challenging issues of social identity, prejudice, and discrimination. Homogenous groups do not preclude diversity dialogue groups: They operate simultaneously, and people can choose which form they prefer. Individuals may choose one type of group and then move to another. Any form that enables people to talk about themselves and their children is useful. John details his thinking on this topic:

I decided to begin the CSDC's initial diversity dialogue group by personally inviting parents from marginalized social–cultural groups in the community where the center is located. I also invited overt allies of the anti-bias mission. I thought it was more important at first to ensure a critical mass of group members committed to a dialogue about bias and equity rather than opening the dialogue group to everyone and risking diverting attention to the concerns of families less comfortable with an anti-bias approach.

Debbie talks about forming a group that shared similarity in identity or family issues at the EPCS:

We formed a support group specifically for families who had children with special needs. Being an inclusion school, we soon found that other families also had questions about children with learning differences. In response, we opened up the group to friends and families of children with special needs. The school's Special Needs Coordinator and a parent facilitated this group, which met monthly on topics including advocacy, the special education IEP process, managing transitions, and the issues for siblings of a child with special needs.

Families as Allies of Anti-Bias Education

I used to think that showing my anti-bias attitude meant not highlighting or bringing up difference, but I've learned that discussing and celebrating these differences in a more active way can be a powerful tool against bias.

—Parent

Identifying family members who can become advocates and allies for anti-bias education at your program begins with the reading of the program (see Chapter 3). As the year progresses, there are several forms that family advocacy and leadership might take.

Families Advocating for Differences. Some differences in a family's social identity are less identifiable than others. Skin color, language, and physical disabilities, such as Down syndrome, are typically more discernable—but not always. Families may deliberately hide some of who they are out of concern about acceptance. Some differences, such as emotional and behavioral challenges, can be hard for community members to comprehend because families do not feel able to share them openly. In an anti-bias community, one of the goals is to support families to feel visible and audible in the community and be able to express all aspects of their identity.

One strategy to achieve this is requesting families, if they are willing, to write a letter to the community about their child's differences, whether obvious or not. This process empowers the family to take ownership and frame the child's differences and abilities in the way they want. This kind of sharing requires a lot of trust and some families may not be ready to make this step, especially if they are still coming to terms with the difference themselves. Other families often become more empathetic once they understand the child's situation and challenges and the ways they can provide support. We have found that this kind of sharing (and visibility) helps to "normalize" and celebrate differences in the community. Typically these types of letters have been used to describe children with special needs, but can also be used to address family circumstances such as adoption and foster care. If a family wants to write a letter to the community about their child's difference, you should welcome that, but do not assume every parent will want to participate.

Figure 5.3 provides a sample letter written to the classroom families by the parents of a child with Down syndrome.

Family Leadership and Initiative. You can promote anti-bias leadership by being intentional about inviting parents to serve on program advisory boards, governance councils, and hiring, outreach, and fundraising committees. You can also include families, along with teachers, in panel presentations at program

Figure 5.3. Sample Letter from the Parents of a Child with Down Syndrome

Dear Families,

We are the parents of Matthew, your child's classmate at the center. Thank you for your warm welcome. Like all parents we have been anxious about our son starting school, and your openness and kindness have helped us feel easier.

We are looking forward to coming in this Thursday to speak with the class about Down syndrome and what this means specifically for our son. Matthew was born with Down syndrome and it is something unique to him. It makes him who he is just as each of your children have things that make him or her unique. Matthew likes to play cars, dance, sing, and read books, just like his friends. However, he approaches these activities differently than most do and needs extra help and time learning to do all of them. As with everyone, there are things he is really good at and there are things that are frustrating and challenging. Like any parent we want our child to be confident and proud of who he is.

We also feel charged to share with others about Down syndrome and to provide current and accurate information. Since Matthew was born, we have learned a lot. We have also learned that many people have questions but are hesitant to ask. We are always open to answering any questions that you or your child has. The center has a variety of resources and books too. Please feel free to contact us anytime.

Sincerely,
Matthew's family

---

meetings and external conferences. John funded a team at his program that included an administrator, a teacher, and a parent of a child with special needs to attend an inclusion leadership meeting at the state capital. He also selected parents for staff hiring committees in order to ensure a diversity of perspectives, as he explains:

Over the years I was proactive about including parents who came from underrepresented groups in the community in various leadership roles. These opportunities to be involved in decision making not only shared power with a broader range of perspectives but also sent a concrete message that all voices were valued. On a hiring committee, we (teachers, parents, and administrators) came to know each other both professionally and personally as we discussed the values and teacher attributes that were most important in an anti-bias program. Parents were able to see the thought and commitment that teachers had for an inclusive program, and we built relationships with allies among our parents.

I realized it was important to be alert for family leadership opportunities that can emerge from programwide activities. For instance, after seeing how engaged some parents were at a parent and teacher lecture on dual-language learners, I personally encouraged four parents (all of whom were on the advisory board and had first languages other than English) to organize and facilitate a follow-up conversation specifically for families with children learning two or more languages. The meeting proceeded without my involvement (other than organizing time, space, child care, and food) and resulted in a set of recommendations and questions that were shared with teachers.

We recommend that you encourage family initiative and leadership by including families in advisory roles whenever possible. Families (and teachers) can be on a hiring committee, help develop policies, and provide input on committees. However, you are ultimately accountable for the bottom line and alignment with the program mission and values. Your role is to shepherd the anti-bias mission, and you need to be clear about why, when, and in what ways you can truly share decision-making power with families, as Debbie's story illustrates:

During one of my first years at the EPCS, a parent came to me about wanting to hold a Halloween parade throughout the school and into the surrounding university campus. I thought this could be a helpful dialogue and opportunity for the whole school, and I offered to take up the topic at the advisory board meeting with all the parents and teachers in attendance. The meeting was one of our best-attended sessions, and the topic generated many emotions. Some people felt holidays were important traditions; they just wanted to have some fun and take photos. Other people, including the majority of teachers, felt it was not developmentally appropriate, that children would be afraid, and that it was feeding into the materialism of the holiday.

Through the dialogue it became evident that for many families it was about *their* desire to do a Halloween parade and not because the children wanted it. Others brought up the point that some people do not celebrate Halloween and that would make them uncomfortable. After the meeting a small group of teachers and parents drafted their ideas into a new holiday policy. I reviewed the final policy before it became part of the family handbook. Below are some key points about holidays that became part of the formal holiday policy.

- Find a balanced approach to holidays without exaggerating the experience or ignoring it.
- Any holiday experience in the school needs to be meaningful to the children and developmentally appropriate, and foster understanding and respect for one another.
- Recognize similarities and celebrate differences. Group holiday celebrations according to the seasons, and look for parallels across cultures; set holiday activities in the context of people's daily lives and beliefs; and connect them to specific children, families, and staff.
- Families are welcome to share their special traditions.
- Listen carefully and respond to children's comments, questions, and feelings about holidays.

FAMILIES ARE MULTIFACETED

Engaging families and growing anti-bias partnerships requires many-sided and versatile strategies. They include creating family visibility and connection, anti-bias education that brings together staff and families, and support systems and opportunities for mentoring of family leadership. As program leader, you should use and adapt strategies and activities that match the needs and dynamics of the particular group of families with whom you work.

Another crucial task of an anti-bias leader is fostering the teachers' knowledge and skills for creating positive relationships and partnerships with the families whose children they serve. In the next chapter, we look at the issues and strategies for doing this important work, as well as other ways that you can continue to deepen the teachers' capacity for anti-bias education.

CHAPTER 6

Deepening and Sustaining Anti-Bias Awareness, Knowledge, and Skills

There is dedicated time to do the work. I have been able to talk about anti-bias issues to my classroom team, and to bring dilemmas to staff meetings and to my supervision meeting with the director. There are many professional development spaces for anti-bias discussion!

—Teacher

The demands of the anti-bias journey call for reflective practitioners, continually assessing where they are and where they want to go next. Accordingly you should continue to generate opportunities throughout the year for your staff's growth in knowledge of anti-bias education, critical reflection on practice, and skills in teaching and working with families. The strategies and activities in this chapter assume that there is now a solid core of teachers who are ready to move forward with the next steps in realizing your anti-bias mission.

In this chapter we pick up where Chapter 4 ended and begin by presenting several professional development strategies for integrating, deepening, and sustaining anti-bias work. Then we build on the theme of Chapter 5 and consider what program leaders can do to facilitate teachers' collaborative work with families.

ENHANCING THE PROFESSIONAL DEVELOPMENT OF ANTI-BIAS TEACHERS

One of the challenges of leading the professional development of an early childhood staff is offering activities that scaffold the varying levels of awareness, knowledge, and skills. The same goes for anti-bias professional development efforts. Not only do adults learn and engage with change in different ways, they also join a team of staff at different points in time and bring with them varying kinds of experience. Your initial "reading" of the program (Chapter 3) and ongoing documentation (Chapter 8) will guide you in making appropriate choices of professional development experiences and strategies that are best matched to your staff's readiness for anti-bias education. Inevitably, you will need to cycle back to the strategies shared in Chapter 4 when you have new staff enter the program or you feel a need to revisit and strengthen foundational ABE concepts.

In the following sections we look at ways you can support teachers at various points in their anti-bias journey, and more specifically those who are eager for deeper levels of involvement and collaboration. First, we consider your role in supporting staff to identify potential anti-bias curriculum and plan for their classrooms. We then discuss how you can engage in supervision, coaching, and mentoring of your teachers around anti-bias goals, and finally outline various professional development modalities you can use to support anti-bias work.

Integrate Anti-Bias Education Into the Daily Curriculum

Our curriculum was so much more responsive with an anti-bias perspective. It became an intentional and explicit way to help our students as we explore our social, emotional, and cultural selves.

—Teacher

Once teachers have a foundational understanding of what anti-bias education encompasses and have begun implementing specific strategies, you should focus on expanding their ability to fully integrate ABE into the ongoing curriculum. The goal is to ensure that teachers reach beyond simply implementing activities from a curriculum guide, no matter how well constructed, by challenging them to think about the particular group of children and families with whom they work at any given time.

Identifying Potential Curriculum. While the four anti-bias core goals form the curriculum framework, specific learning opportunities and activities arise from the observed needs, questions, and backgrounds of the children in any particular program (Jones & Nimmo, 1994). Your ongoing observation of classrooms provides an opportunity to engage teachers in thinking about children's questions, comments, and responses regarding diversity and to help them identify starting points for specific anti-bias curriculum themes and activities. Your objective is to help teachers brainstorm ways to build on a child's specific comment or interaction by planning ways to explore the issue with the whole group. Thinking about curriculum together in this way reinforces the daily, ongoing, and emergent nature of opportunities to build anti-bias curriculum. For instance, the teacher has put out play dough in several skin tones from light to dark brown. One of the children picks up a darker brown piece of play dough, says, "his one is yucky; I don't like it," and throws it down. Other children imitate him. Happening to observe this incident, the program leader tells the teacher about it during a lull in the action. After thinking about possible underlying reasons for the first child's behavior, the teacher decides to create a variety of learning opportunities over the next week to enable all the children to explore skin colors, learn the purposes of the color in skin, and gain appreciation for the beauty of all skin colors. The teacher also plans to listen carefully to further comments from the children, to better understand their thinking and to help her develop further activities as needed.

Sometimes the provocation for curriculum may come from an event outside of the classroom. Your role is to help teachers make the potential anti-bias connection to the event. John tells this story to illustrate how you can support a teacher in identifying an opportunity to explore values and beliefs regarding social-economic class with children. In this example, the objective was to help the children become more aware of *all* the members of their community:

I asked a facilities employee to look at a piece of rotting wood on our tree house while he was at the center fixing a door. He went out of his way to replace the wood, so I asked the teachers to invite the children to share their thoughts about what he had done in making their house available again for play. They wrote thank-you letters with pictures and posted them off to him. My thinking was that the children could appreciate that there are many people who work hard (often after hours) to ensure the center is clean and maintained—that it's not magic—it requires skill and hard work. I shared my reasoning with the worker, and he appreciated being valued and welcomed. This issue had been part of a larger discussion with teachers about auxiliary staff being more visible in our community. The teachers talked about trying to be more cognizant of when facilities workers were at the center. Rather than seeing them as a disruption or having nothing to do with the curriculum, they realized that they could say to the children, "This is Louisa—she's here to help get rid of the wasps. Let's say thank-you to Louisa for doing that!"

Planning Guide for Teachers. Using the following steps for developing learning experiences helps teachers think through, in a more systematic way, how to implement anti-bias education with their particular group of children. This guide is an adapted version of a teacher's framework used at the Eliot–Pearson Children's School (Kuh, Beneke, LeeKeenan, & Given, in press).

Step 1. Observation/Documentation: Data Gathering

- What are the children saying in their conversations with each other and teachers? What are the children asking about or showing us through their play and actions?
- What are families talking about?
- What topics are in the children's environment?
- What are teachers thinking about?
- Given your observations/documentation, what are the possible entry points for doing anti-bias curriculum?

Step 2. Reflection: Teachers share and analyze their data together, both in staff meetings and in individual meetings with the program leader.

- What are the issues that emerge from the children?
- What are the emotions behind these issues for children?
- What are some questions and topics that might be of interest and developmentally/culturally appropriate to explore with children?
- What issues and feelings arise for teachers and for families in relation to the identified issues for the children?

Step 3. Curriculum Response: Learning experiences that address, explore, and expand on the children's questions and issues.

- What are our criteria for choosing specific topics to explore?
- Given a specific topic, how could we respond in the moment, generate learning experiences in the long term, and revisit or expand a topic with children?
- How do we implement curriculum that supports different kinds of learning styles?
- How do we make the topic accessible and concrete for children?

Step 4. Assessment

- What worked and didn't work? Why?
- What have we learned with and about the children?
- What have we learned about ourselves? What was challenging?
- How do we share with families and our colleagues what we have done in the classroom?
- How do we solicit feedback from the children, families, and other staff in the community?
- Where do we go from here?

Schoolwide Curriculum Anti-Bias Focus. Another strategy for integrating anti-bias perspective into the classroom is to implement a schoolwide curriculum on a particular topic. This approach draws on the resources of your entire staff and encourages both peer mentoring and greater sharing of what classrooms are doing in their anti-bias curriculum.

Topics that provoke anti-bias questions could be anything that can lend itself to looking at similarities and differences. For example, the topic of shelters/homes could be the curriculum topic. All people have a right to some form of shelter, but each is different, and not everyone has the shelter they need. Some shelters are permanent, some are temporary. Some people live in a house, an apartment, a condo, a tent, a multifamily house, a houseboat, a motel, or a car. What makes a shelter a home? Each classroom could study shelters, read books about shelters, and make shelters out of blocks, sticks, cardboard boxes, and other materials.

Debbie describes another curriculum example:

> At the EPCS, we conducted a schoolwide curriculum about anti-bias topics. Each classroom focused on a "social identity category"—the 3-year-old class focused on family diversity, the 4-year-old group focused on racial identity, the kindergarten focused on class and privilege, the 1st/2nd grade focused on ability differences, and the afternoon mixed-age group focused on home culture and language [see Chapter 8 for information on how this curriculum was documented and shared].

In any kind of schoolwide curriculum there are four key points to remember:

- Choose a topic that has potential for all age groups and can be explored in multiple ways.
- Provide opportunities (e.g., at staff meetings) for educators from across the program to meet regularly to share, plan, and problem-solve together. These conversations become effective professional development experiences.
- Encourage family participation in the curriculum by sharing the topic with families and getting their ideas, questions, and concerns right in the beginning. Some anti-bias topics are controversial for programs, such as talking about religious beliefs or the distribution of wealth. Allowing families to raise their concerns in the beginning is being proactive (see Chapter 7 for how to deal with conflicts that may arise). Teachers can hold an end-of-the-investigation celebration where children share what they learned. At these events teachers have some of the curriculum activities for families to try out. For example, at EPCS, families had the opportunity to mix their own skin-color paints, and make their own self-portraits using the paints, just like the children did as part of the racial-identity study.
- A schoolwide newsletter on the topic is one way to share what is happening in the classrooms with families across the school. Each classroom writes an article about their particular classroom; the program leader writes about why this topic is important to young children and includes a section on resources and children's books on the topic.

Supervise and Coach Teachers in Anti-Bias Work

Through supervision and coaching, you have a direct, continuing opportunity to influence a teacher's anti-bias growth. Supervision and coaching work hand in hand. You use positive and critical feedback, ask provocation questions, and scaffold suggestions to help teachers move to a new step in their work. Individual supervision meetings are safe places to discuss and support a teacher's professional goals and needs. You should intentionally scaffold how you work with teachers, taking into account the stage of each teacher on the anti-bias journey. Finding the point where each individual can move to a next step, but not be pushed into too much disequilibrium, is key.

While supervision and coaching teachers are an essential part of your responsibilities, how you organize these sessions depends on the characteristics, dynamics, and needs of the program. These include, but are not limited to, size of staff, number of staff per classroom, and time you have in the face of all responsibilities. Debbie explains how she handled supervision at EPCS:

I held regular (weekly or biweekly) individual supervision meetings with the five head teachers. They came prepared with their agenda, questions they had about curriculum, children, or families. I responded to and supported the teacher, and also introduced appropriate scaffolding and resources, based on what I assessed that particular teacher needed. I learned when to challenge a specific teacher to the "next level," and when I needed to hold back for a bit. I based these decisions on my knowledge of the teacher's readiness, resiliency, and abilities. Sometimes I provided a prompt or focus for the teacher to implement (e.g., Keep track of who plays in the dramatic play area and block area. Is it just boys or girls? Why do you think that happens? Is it something you want to shift? What can you do?).

Conducting regular observation of teachers was another way I supported and coached staff. I held a preconference with the teacher, asking questions such as, "How can this observation help you? What do you want feedback on?" For example, the teacher might ask if she is using different language with the boys and girls in the block area. Sometimes I initiated an observation session; sometimes a teacher requested an observation of a learning experience about which he wanted feedback. During an observation, I took notes on what was working, including specific language the teacher used, actions about which I had questions, and noted suggestions for improvement. During the postobservation conversation, I asked the teacher how she felt the lesson went (What went well? What would you change?) before I gave my feedback.

Model Anti-Bias Teaching in the Classroom

Your going into the classroom to model working with the children on a specific piece of anti-bias curriculum demonstrates to the teacher how to make complex ideas developmentally appropriate and how to stimulate children to think about a specific anti-bias issue. You can also model teaching an anti-bias activity when a teacher is unsure about how to handle an anti-bias issue. Modeling gives you and the teachers a common experience to reflect on together during supervision meetings. Teachers can then do follow-up activities with the children in ensuing days. It also emphasizes the importance you give to this work and models risk taking. Debbie notes:

At the beginning of each year, I visited each classroom to read one of my favorite books that focuses on diversity. With teachers less familiar with ABE, I might read a book such as *Bread, Bread, Bread* (Morris, 1993), which has photographs of people all over the world eating different types of bread. The anti-bias theme is about similarities and differences in how people living in diverse cultural settings make and eat food—some are like what the children's families do and some are different. We discuss questions such as: What do you notice about the different types of breads? How do you think they are made? What types of grain are the breads made from? What kinds of bread do you and your families like to eat? How are these similar or different from breads you are seeing in the book? I also encouraged the children to ask questions about the similarities and differences they notice in the people and settings in the photographs. Next, I brought samples of different types of bread (challah, manto, steamed bread, and tortillas) to taste. Over the next several weeks the teacher might then do bread baking and invite different families to come to the classroom to share the type of bread they eat in their homes.

The program leader can also use modeling to help teachers consider a more effective way to teach about a specific topic. Debbie shares a story about introducing the topic of Rosa Parks and the Montgomery Bus Boycott as a way to recognize the Dr. Martin Luther King Jr. national holiday.

The EPCS teachers wondered how to implement curriculum about Rosa Parks and the Montgomery Bus Boycott that would be meaningful to young children. I mentioned that I grew up during the civil rights movement and would be happy to share my powerful memories of this time with the children. This evolved into my telling the story of Rosa Parks and Montgomery Bus Boycott [Clemens, 1988] with the children taking on roles to help tell the story. We wanted to use the story of the bus boycott as a provocation that leads children to think more deeply about social justice as it pertains to everyday life.

I began with giving the children a context for this story. "This story takes place during a time when I was a little girl and the laws were very different than they are now. People who had brown skin and people who had white skin could not be together— they had to go to separate schools, eat in separate restaurants, play in different playgrounds, and even drink from different water fountains. I thought this was very unfair, and it made me angry and sad that there were laws like that. Today I am going to tell you a story about two people who helped change those unfair laws. Their names are Dr. King and Rosa Parks, and they are my heroes." After making this personal connection to the bus boycott story, I invited all the children to act out the Rosa Parks and Bus Boycott incident. As I narrated the story, the children acted it out. We later acted out a Montgomery Improvement Association community meeting, led by Dr. King, where the children brainstormed ideas to the question, "What can you do when something is unfair?" We talked more about what a boycott is and then pantomimed "walking and walking" to boycott the unfair laws, rather than riding the bus. Afterward the children had an opportunity to make buses out of construction paper and show where people would sit on the bus before and after the laws were changed. Eventually the director's coming to each classroom to act out the Rosa Parks story became a yearly tradition at EPCS, to which the children and teachers looked forward.

The program leader uses these opportunities to model the importance of carefully thinking through the complexities of anti-bias curriculum. For instance, there are some cautions to keep in mind with the Rosa Parks activity, even if it is one that would be meaningful to the children in your setting. One is to be careful to make clear that anyone can play any role—do not assign roles by the skin color of the children. Another is to inform families about the activity, as they may have questions and children may want to discuss it at home. Also, in dealing with historical events it is important that you ensure that the children know that this particular unfairness happened a long time ago and that the rules have changed. Finally, this activity should not be a singular event, but one of many that discuss unfairness, fairness, and taking action to fix unfair behaviors and situations that occur in the children's own life.

In the end, modeling anti-bias teaching rests on choosing activities that make sense for the backgrounds and developmental levels of the specific children and teachers with whom you work. Is this an anti-bias concept that would appropriately challenge the teacher? Does this concept and content make sense given the children's backgrounds and developmental level?

Mentor Leadership Capacity of Teachers

Leaders build teacher capacity and ability to take the initiative in anti-bias education through a process of mentoring over time. At John's and Debbie's programs, they encouraged teachers to participate in leadership opportunities and used these as occasions to mentor their skills and dispositions. Mentorship involves a supportive relationship of careful guidance for teachers in which you ask questions, provide expertise, and engage in dialogue. This relationship continues in the many one-on-one and more personal interactions that you have with teachers throughout the day.

Leadership Groups. These groups may be a mentor or representative teacher group, a schoolwide diversity task force (including family representatives), or a family advisory board team. The program leader might send a leadership group to a conference, diversity workshop, or special training, with the expectation that the leadership group would share what they learned with the rest of the staff. This could be through a presentation to the whole staff, distributing handouts and summary notes, and meetings with the others in their particular stakeholder group.

As mentioned earlier, John initiated the Diversity, Equity, and Bias Task Force (DEBT) at the CSDC:

I asked five teachers who had begun to raise questions regarding diversity, to commit to participating on the task force for 2 years. The group met monthly during school time, beginning with concrete tasks such as reviewing the intake questionnaire, before moving on to development of a diversity mission statement [refer to Figure 4.1]. This taskforce was an occasion for me to challenge perspectives in a way that was difficult in larger all-staff meetings. I expected committee members to take responsibility for raising diversity issues in their team meetings with peers. Over a number of years, the group read books together, developed guidelines on anti-bias issues for the staff, facilitated anti-bias workshops, and hosted a series of evening forums for families we called "Diversity Dialogues." Later we branched out with a second key task force focused on the inclusion of children with varying abilities. This group of teachers engaged in similar activities to DEBT and created an inclusion action plan for the center.

Cross-Program Study Groups. Setting up study groups with a combination of staff, teachers, and families is another way to grow anti-bias work. These groups encourage individual teachers and family members to take leadership as meeting planners and facilitators. Then program leaders move into the role of colearner. At EPCS, each study group consisted of 6–10 staff and family members, with staff and parent cofacilitators planning and convening the evening sessions. Cross-study groups (some of which focus on topics other than anti-bias ones) can meet a wide range of needs in a program; new topics may also emerge over the course of the year. Some groups may become a support group for the participants; others may work as action groups on behalf of the whole school community (e.g., sponsoring a schoolwide diversity speaker or creating a resource binder on anti-bias resources for families).

Provide Multiple Opportunities for Learning Together About ABE

There are several ways for the program leader to create experiences for staff to begin or continue their anti-bias professional development. You should differentiate the experiences to meet the needs of your staff. The following are familiar professional strategies in the ECCE field, but the content, specific approaches, and the role of the program leader are designed to support an anti-bias mission.

Staff Meetings. Regular meetings about curriculum development and teaching offer a central place to build an anti-bias learning community. While you ensure that anti-bias issues are included on the agenda, it's important to involve staff in planning the specific agenda items as a way to distribute power and encourage individuals to take more ownership of the proceedings. Anti-Bias growth requires that participants actively engage in the process of change.

At staff meetings teachers can routinely share documentation of their classroom anti-bias work. These may include stories about children, issues, challenges, questions, and effective—as well as missed—learning opportunities. Their colleagues' feedback and discussions provide support and teaching ideas, which help teachers improve their classroom practice. These staff meetings also play a key role in creating a learning community that allows for risk taking, critical reflection, and growth.

In their programs Debbie and John organized a system of professional learning communities where different teaching teams signed up for a particular staff meeting and shared a specific question or dilemma they had that could include anti-bias issues from their classroom. The teachers brought photos, a work sample, short video clip, or transcript of a conversation to the staff meeting. After viewing the documentation and hearing the teacher's questions, the rest of the group had a discussion about the issues. To help structure such conversations, specific protocols from the School Reform Initiative (see www. schoolreforminitiative.org/) are useful. As leader, you could share issues that come up for you as well, modeling the kind of communication anti-bias education work requires.

An alternative approach is to engage the teachers themselves in a specific anti-bias education activity that is intended for children, and then talk together about what children can learn from the activity. For example, the teachers could make an "all about brown group collage," working together with a range of beautiful brown materials (e.g., cinnamon, pinecones, pine needles, sand, silk fabrics, feathers, spices). After discussing what the children might learn from an activity like this, you can review child development issues. For example, some children have negative associations with dark colors, and many begin to connect negative associations with dark skin during the preschool years (Ramsey, 2004). Anti-Bias educators need to counteract those stereotypes.

Assigned Readings. You can give the staff a shared reading to complete for a discussion group, meeting, or retreat. This may be an article, a book (fiction or nonfiction), or chapter from a book that matches the literacy level of the staff members and can be completed in the time available. If time is limited, shorter readings or excerpts of 2–5 pages that the staff can read *during* the meeting may be in order, or provide the reading as a supplemental resource after the meeting.

The purpose of the reading is to provide a common knowledge base that everyone can then discuss in the whole group or in small groups. You can use prompts such as these: What did this mean to you? How does it apply to anti-bias work? What is your take-away message from the book? Readings can explore any aspect of social identity, diversity, bias, equity, and social justice education (see Appendix A for a list of resources, available at www.tcpress. com).

Workshops. Part- or full-day workshops with outside facilitators are useful as occasional activities. They can introduce new topics with which they have experience and that you may not feel ready to offer to staff by yourself. They also help staff see how the work at their center connects to a bigger context, allow you to be a learner along with the staff, and reinforce concepts and content that staff is exploring. An outside workshop facilitator may be a teacher or program leader from another center, an anti-bias educator at a nearby community college or university, a local diversity/social justice leader, or family and community members talking about values and childrearing practices from their cultural background. For example, during his second year as director, John invited Debbie to come to the CSDC to lead an anti-bias training:

As friends and colleagues, Debbie and I had already begun to develop relationships between our staffs. Teachers from her center had visited us, and vice versa. Some teachers from both centers had presented at a conference together, so there were personal and collegial connections. She wasn't simply an outsider. Second, I felt Debbie would not be confrontational. She makes folks feel comfortable, is very down-to-earth and concrete in her delivery, but still stretches folks' thinking. I wanted this to engage everyone in a joyful way and get their juices running—to be excited about the work not dreading it! Third, Debbie is a woman of color and comfortable, open, and clear about her identity. I knew she would project this to staff. In many ways, inviting Debbie was an important turning point in engaging all the staff in a more concrete conversation about how to implement our anti-bias commitment in the classroom.

Keep in mind, that while occasional workshops by outside experts are a useful part of an anti-bias professional development plan, they do not take the place of ongoing professional development facilitated by the program leader.

Staff Retreats. Staff retreats provide a concentrated time to focus on specific aspects of professional development and on community building, away from the distractions of daily teaching. They differ from regular staff meetings, which usually occur after a long day with children, for 1–2 hours, and with many different agenda items to cover. Staff retreats are ideal for focusing on anti-bias work as there is more time to really immerse in in-depth conversations. Some retreats begin with a guest speaker and then small-group discussion and planning follow.

Attending Professional Conferences. Allocating release time and funds for educators to attend targeted conferences to learn about diversity and equity beyond their own classroom and program educates and reinforces their own efforts. When two or more teachers attend together, it allows for personal reflection and trust. It also creates a higher likelihood that learning from the conference will transfer to the rest of the staff. Encouraging educators to present their ideas at a conference is also an empowering experience. Doing this as a team, where you and teachers present together is a good way to mentor them to gain the confidence and skills they need to disseminate what they know and do. As mentioned in Chapter 5, adding interested family members to a conference presentation enhances their involvement in your anti-bias efforts. Let us now expand the discussion of professional development to focus on teacher–family interactions.

FACILITATING TEACHERS' WORK WITH FAMILIES

Trying to make different members of the community feel respected when their beliefs are in contradiction to my own or others' is difficult.

—Teacher

Program leaders also facilitate teachers effectively reaching out to and interacting with all families. This section describes several professional development strategies for strengthening teachers' work with families on anti-bias issues, which build on to those shared in Chapter 5.

Support Critical Self-Assessment

You should assess how comfortable and familiar teachers are with families who come from different backgrounds and social identities, and then determine ways to help teachers stretch outside their comfort zones. In addition, facilitate their critical reflection and problem solving about their conversations and interactions with families.

Professional development about families is integrated into ongoing anti-bias work with staff, including individual supervision meetings, staff meetings, and professional development workshops, as mentioned in the previous section of this chapter.

Anti-Bias Self-Study Guide. This tool, developed by Chen, Nimmo, and Fraser (2009), is discussed in detail in Chapter 8 and provided in Appendix B, which is available online at www.tcpress.com. The guide has a section on "relationships with families and communities" with questions that are a helpful starting place for teachers to self-assess how they feel about working with families. Based on how each staff member responds to these questions, you can identify individual professional goals and plan relevant professional development trainings (see Chapter 4 for examples).

Unpacking the Ghosts at the Table. Sarah Lawrence-Lightfoot (2003) studied parents' and teachers' perspectives on parent–teacher conferences and discusses how everyone brings previous histories with schooling to the present, whether those were positive or negative experiences. Lightfoot calls this the "ghosts" at the conference table. Parents' previous experiences influence their expectations for their children now. Teachers also need to be aware of their own baggage and how this may interfere with how they relate to families. One way to address this issue is to have teachers and families share their own personal schooling stories with each other.

For example, at the Eliot-Pearson Children's School, curriculum night is one of the first times that families gather each year (without children) to meet with teachers. As an icebreaker activity, families and staff members introduce themselves by sharing their memories of their first school experience:

- What kind of school did you go to and what age?
- What do you remember about the teacher?
- What role did your family have in school?

As you know, families come from a wide range of previous school experiences: urban, rural, private, traditional, schools where many languages are spoken, and so on. There will also be a range of responses, from happy memories where teachers or families remember the play dough or special snack they had, to emotional stories about feeling abandoned and crying all day because they missed their parents. The discussion may be about how it felt to be left at school, how the parent must have felt, and how the teacher handled the crying. You can then discuss how these memories influence how parents handle separation with their own children or the strategies the teacher may use in the classroom.

Their history and expectations also influence how families look at the role of the teacher. For example, in some cultures home and school are seen as separate worlds:

- It is not the role of the family to come into the classroom and read a story or do a cooking project.
- The parent's role is at home or making a living.
- Family members are not trained or educated to be "a teacher" and should not be in the classroom.

Some teachers may not be aware of these cultural norms and assume that particular families are not involved in school life because they are "not interested." Your task is to help teachers unpack the conversations and interactions, not make assumptions, in order to better support families.

Fears About Engaging Families. Teachers may feel uncomfortable, and nervous about how to respond to questions or concerns parents have about anti-bias issues. As the leader, let teachers know that you are a resource and will back them up when needed. They need to know that it is okay to make a mistake or misspeak as part of their learning process. Their anxiety about specific topics often reflects the teachers' identity and personal experiences. But some topics, like sex and religion, are typically touchy subjects for any teacher because of views about the boundaries between parent and school responsibilities.

You should look for the balance between supporting teachers starting where they are comfortable and challenging them to take more risks with curriculum and conversation. When controversial conversations occur between children in the classroom, it is critical for the teacher to share this with families, either with the individual families of the children involved or with the whole class in a newsletter or meeting. The purpose is to let families know how the teacher is handling the challenging topic and the curriculum response being planned, and to allow families an opportunity to share questions or concerns. You can talk the teacher through this process of responding (by asking questions and offering suggestions and resources) or even by being present at a meeting. Debbie recalls her experience related to handling a challenging topic:

I offered to participate in potentially challenging parent–teacher conferences. One time during our supervision meeting, a teacher shared with me that she overheard a set of twins in her preschool classroom talking about their family using the words "surrogate, egg donor, two daddies." The teacher thought the language the children were using among themselves should be shared with their family. We discussed that it would be important to first meet with the two dads of the twins to find out what language they use at home. The teacher requested I also join the meeting, since this could be potentially controversial. The teacher was worried that the two dads would think the school was challenging the choice of words they used at home with their children. In the end the teacher was comfortable leading the meeting, but my support to preview the situation with her and then just to be in the room provided her with additional confidence. The two dads appreciated the opportunity to share about their family, and the teacher and dads eventually drafted a letter (that I reviewed) that went out to all families about the language the children use.

Sharing Your Identity. An anti-bias approach requires staff members to build awareness of their social identities (see Chapter 4). This enables them to be more conscious of the impact of identity on perceptions of and interactions with families who may share both similarities and differences. Sharing experiences relating to one's social identities with families can demonstrate a willingness to talk about and embrace differences. It can also enable educators to better connect and empathize with families in their program, particularly those feeling marginalized. Typically, traditional notions of professionalism give implicit permission for staff to share areas of identity that reflect mainstream values and culture, while often keeping other aspects less visible. For instance, a teacher who is heterosexual happily shares news of her upcoming wedding, while a teacher who is lesbian may feel pressure not to share similar news. A Muslim staff member decides not to share with families that he is fasting and taking time off to celebrate Ramadan, while families and staff freely talk about holiday plans for the "Christmas" break. A teacher who is stressed and late one morning because she can't afford to get her car fixed does not share her predicament with families, while a teacher who is jet-lagged from a vacation trip draws empathy from parents.

Healthy relationship-building between ECCE staff and families requires a comfortable and ongoing exchange about who they are in the world. Program leaders can model and show support for staff to share their identities with the school community in appropriate ways that respect confidentiality and agreed-upon professional boundaries. Setting these boundaries can be complex and entails dialogue and mindfulness about the values and goals of an anti-bias approach.

Further Skills for Interacting with Families

Staff members need coaching on effective skills for interacting with families in culturally responsive ways. You should model these techniques as well as provide professional development opportunities for teachers to learn these skills.

What, How, and When to Ask. Given the multidimensional nature of working with diverse families, it is important for teachers to be open and get as much information as they can about a child's background as soon as possible. As discussed in Chapter 5, teachers can undertake this process during the intake process, home visits, parent–teacher conferences, and ongoing dialogue. The information can be gathered verbally or in writing. Open-ended as well as specific questions are helpful. Some examples include:

- Tell me about your child (temperament, personality, interests, abilities).
- What are your child's favorite toys or activities?
- Are there any activities your child avoids?
- Describe your child's sleeping schedule.
- Describe your child's eating patterns; what are his or her favorite foods?
- What languages does your child speak at home? What languages does your child hear at home?
- What cultural and religious holidays, celebration or traditions, do you practice at home? Are there any that you would be willing to share with us at school?
- What are your expectations for your child?
- What are your aspirations, dreams, and hopes for your child?
- Is there anything else you would like us to know about your child or family (traditions, cultural background, race, religion, home language, culture, and family structure)?

Cross-Cultural Communication. You should ensure the teachers understand cross-cultural communication. Communication between people from different backgrounds is very complex because of the inseparability of language and culture. We mean more than speaking different languages. Nonverbal communication, such as eye contact, proximity, touch, facial expressions, body positions, and gestures, can mean different things for different social and cultural groups. Providing resources, such as *Developing Cross-Cultural Competence: A Guide for Working with Children and Their Families* (Lynch & Hanson, 2011) and *Look at Me When I Talk to You* (Helmer & Eddy, 2012), can help staff become aware of and understand these differences. Through your ongoing supervision and professional development, staff can develop cross-cultural communication skills including:

- Identifying their own communication code
- Taking time to listen more carefully
- Paying attention to details
- Suspending judgment and considering alternatives
- Developing empathy
- Feeling relaxed with families who may be different from themselves

Cultural Conflicts. When teachers and parents come from different cultural backgrounds, there is the risk that teachers will not recognize or understand the social values underlying children's behaviors and a family's childrearing styles. It is vital for teachers early on to be aware of potential areas of conflict so they can be proactive in supporting the children and family. Likewise, families may misunderstand program policies and teacher actions because of differences in cultural values (York, 2003). Common areas of cultural conflict include the following:

- Discipline and child guidance techniques
- Gender roles and expectations
- Age-related expectations of children
- Children's learning approaches
- Sleep and bedtime routines
- Mealtime behavior and diet
- Child's responsibilities at home
- Health and safety
- Attachment and separation
- Views about the role of teachers and schools
- The significance of children's play

It is your role to help identify the potential cultural conflicts and support teachers in resolving them. In Chapter 7, we address the issue of disequilibrium and conflict as part of an anti-bias program and suggest guidelines for managing disagreements and working together for solutions that take the needs of all parties into account.

Home Visits. Some programs use home visits as a strategy to get to know children and their families on their own turf. Your task is to make sure teachers are clear about the purpose of the home visit and have the skills for talking with the range of families served by the program.

In an anti-bias approach, teachers also need to be aware that some families may not be okay with a home visit, especially at the beginning of the program year. Some families feel intimidated or anxious about a teacher coming to their home, often because social class and cultural issues come into play. A family may feel the school is coming to the home to check up on them as parents. Some may worry that a home visit is about confirming their legal immigrant status. A family could feel obligated to prepare a huge meal for the teacher as a sign of respect.

Because of these and other reasons, families may prefer to meet at a more neutral setting, like a playground or community center. It may take a long time for families to develop enough trust and comfort with the program to accept a teacher visit at their home.

Documentation can be a way to add a new component to home visits. During home visits, with the family's permission, a teacher could take a photo of the front door of each child's home. By focusing on the door, rather than the entire house or apartment, parents are likely to be more at ease with sharing this aspect of their lives. Back at the program, the teacher and/or children paste each door photo onto the lid of an individual small cardboard box (5x7). The inside of each box is decorated with a photo of the family and a short description of who lives in the house. The collection of "family doors" is then posted on the wall of the classroom or used by children as props (little homes) in the block area. This activity connects the home and program and visually recognizes the range of homes and families in each classroom.

Parent Panel. Opportunities for teachers to hear directly from families about their experiences are particularly effective professional development experiences. One strategy is to create a parent panel for a staff meeting to share their diverse experiences in schools, their hopes and dreams, and their challenges and concerns.

Debbie and John have organized parent panels on topics such as parenting a child with special needs, raising a bilingual child, and home–school partnerships. When creating a parent panel, you should intentionally invite parents who represent a range of perspectives on a specific topic and come from a diversity of backgrounds. Some parents may feel they are not articulate or outgoing enough to be on a panel. You need to be encouraging by assuring the family member that he or she has much to offer the community and staff. Parents find they learn how teachers and other families think by participating on the panel. After the session, you can acknowledge and show gratitude to the participants on the panel by listing their names in the newsletter and writing thank-you notes.

Curriculum Night. You set the expectation that teachers will inform families how they integrate anti-bias education into their classrooms. Debbie suggests two approaches:

At the EPCS the first parent meeting of the year was the fall curriculum night where teachers provided a curriculum overview of the year and what families could expect. As director, I asked that teachers include anti-bias education on the agenda by sharing how the approach is part of the classroom curriculum. Another strategy we tried was for me to open the evening by presenting a 15-minute "keynote" about anti-bias education to families from the whole school. Families then went to their individual classrooms to discuss what anti-bias looked like in their classrooms with the teachers. This strategy ensured that everyone heard the same message but provided small-group and age-specific examples in each classroom.

Use the strategies we suggest for fostering teacher's awareness, knowledge, and skills for working with families on diversity and fairness issues; adapt them to meet the needs of your particular group; or create new ones. In the end, expanding staff's capacity to work effectively with families of all backgrounds will greatly improve the quality of your program in general, and your anti-bias work in particular.

STAFF DEVELOPMENT THROUGHOUT THE YEAR

Scaffolding and supporting the anti-bias professional growth of the adults in your program has its challenges—such as carving out the time and resources to do it throughout the year. At the same time, it is the only way to build and sustain an anti-bias early childhood program. Staff members' growth brings great benefits—for them, and for the children and families your program serves. It will also bring rewards to you, as you watch educators' understanding of themselves and the world evolve and they gain a greater sense of professional confidence, competence, and commitment. Next, we turn to one of the dynamics of anti-bias work that may worry you, yet actually has within it the possibilities for furthering professional development and the quality of your program. In Chapter 7 we examine the issues and strategies for constructively using the inevitable conflict and disequilibrium that is part of anti-bias change.

Managing and Negotiating Disequilibrium and Conflict

Change means movement. Movement means friction. Only in the frictionless vacuum of a nonexistent abstract world can movement or change occur without that abrasive friction of conflict.

—Saul D. Alinsky (1971, p. 21)

Early childhood program leaders worry about the possibilities for conflict if they pursue an anti-bias approach. If they are already underway with their anti-bias efforts, leaders may view disagreements as disruptive, unwelcome, and something to avoid. How a program leader prepares for and responds to conflict situations influences their outcomes. When a leader backs away from conflict, this can stifle progress toward an anti-bias vision.

Anti-Bias work does generate disagreements and dissonance. These dynamics are inevitable as teachers, families, and administrators act on their deeply held and diverse values regarding childrearing and education. Broader contested grounds in ECCE, such as whether schools should have a role in achieving social justice, also fuel these conflicts. Emotional and cognitive disequilibrium often occur in conflict situations, accompanied by a range of feelings such as anger, frustration, and discomfort.

From a constructivist framework, conflict is a productive part of the learning process. The disequilibrium created by conflict is a prelude to problem solving and sharing information, creating opportunities for people to expand and shift their perspectives and behaviors. With this in mind, anti-bias education leaders embrace conflict as a healthy dynamic in the pursuit of change.

We begin this chapter by defining conflict in anti-bias efforts. Then we discuss several strategies for managing conflict situations between various combinations of program stakeholders (e.g., leader, staff, and family members). We examine the procedure of finding the third space as a preferred way to generate discrete solutions to particular conflicts in specific situations. Last, we consider the issue of resistance and opposition to anti-bias work and ways to stay on course.

UNDERSTANDING CONFLICT

Anti-bias education is a complicated, messy process. There is not an easy solution.

—Teacher

Given the focus on building caring relationships in early childhood, many educators focus most of their energy on avoiding conflict and keeping the peace. Anti-bias leadership requires that early childhood professionals reframe how they view the nature and purpose of conflict, as well as the disequilibrium and emotions it evokes. In this section we look at the meaning and dynamics of conflict from this perspective.

Forms of Conflict

Conflicts in anti-bias endeavors occur when there is dissonance between two or more perspectives on a specific equity, diversity, or bias issue. We distinguish three possible forms of conflict among program stakeholders: (1) inner disequilibrium, (2) disagreements, and (3) opposition. All may be part of the change process. Each type also brings different degrees of intensity and discomfort for those involved, as well as possibilities for finding a productive resolution.

Inner Disequilibrium. Conflict can be an inner and very personal struggle. Because anti-bias education shifts the status quo and challenges values and practices, it is inevitable that stakeholders will experience some level of intellectual and emotional disequilibrium, including the leader. It can be an uncomfortable experience to have one's current thinking shaken up. Everyone needs time to consider new information and perspectives. Then, is the reaction to modify and expand thinking or to reject the new ideas? An example comes from Debbie's work at the EPCS involving a family's feedback as they were leaving the program to move on to elementary school. Even though she experienced considerable disequilibrium, Debbie took the time to reflect and learn from the situation, as she explains here:

At the end of one school year, one of the families asked me for a meeting. I assumed they wanted to say good-bye and to thank me for their experiences at the school. While they did express appreciation, they also had something else to say. They told me they had been uncomfortable with our curriculum about families that included books and posters of same-sex families. Specifically, they noted that their religion did not accept same-sex families.

Surprised they were giving me this feedback now, I replied that I wish they had come to me earlier. When one parent asked, "Would you have changed the curriculum?" I knew the answer was no. I told them that and explained that the curriculum represented the diversity of families in the world, and even more important, in our own community. An inclusive family curriculum was an expression of the school's anti-bias mission. I also thanked the parents for telling me their feelings. I want my office and the school to be a safe place for families to express their viewpoints and concerns, even if the outcome is to agree to disagree.

This conversation echoed in my mind long after it was over. It was not an issue of whether or not we should include same-sex families in our curriculum, but I pondered what more I might have done to prepare people for it. I kept thinking about questions such as:

- Could I have presented the idea of the family curriculum differently and tried to find out more about how families felt?
- Did I take into consideration all the family viewpoints?
- How did my own assumptions and values filter my responses both in the decision to have an inclusive family curriculum and to the family when they spoke up?

I concluded that this was an example of a disagreement for which I could not find a solution that made everyone happy. I have noticed that, over time, my emotional responses to such moments of disagreement and disequilibrium have changed. Twenty years ago, I would have felt criticized by the family and disappointed by my inability to please them. I would have wanted to "fix it" in some way to make everyone happy. I also may have felt impatient toward the family for being unable to understand the importance of supporting same-sex families.

Why did the family come to see me in the first place? By openly sharing with me, they might have been looking for some resolution to their own disequilibrium from the tension between their beliefs and their belonging to our anti-bias community. Today, I am less judgmental in my thinking about people with whom I disagree. I try to understand what underlies their positions and empathize with the conflicts they feel. My goal is to try to find common ground, but I can also accept that sometimes that does not happen, and I am at peace with agreeing to disagree. My experience with this family helped me to see that sitting with discomfort and living with disagreements are inevitable facets of anti-bias work.

Program leaders can assume that teachers and families will also experience disequilibrium as they encounter change. Leaders can help create a culture in which staff and families are more comfortable with this disequilibrium around anti-bias issues by using intentional provocations. A provocation may be new information, asking questions, or offering experiences that challenge staff and families to think about an issue in new and unexpected ways. For example, Debbie described the following strategy she used at EPCS:

I challenged staff and family members to become more aware of stereotyping in the media and the world around us. I asked everyone to bring in books, posters, or toys to share at staff and parent meetings and to display (with questions) in the school's entranceway. People brought in provocative items such as wooden block figures that depicted Black people as servants and maids, chopsticks labeled as "chimp sticks" with a monkey at the end, and books with stereotypical illustrations. One teacher shared a package of miniature figures labeled "fat people" purchased from a local toy store. To facilitate discussion, I asked and posted questions such as:

- What is the message this object or image might give your child?
- What is fair or unfair, inaccurate, or hurtful about the message?
- Why or why not would you use this with young children?
- How would you explain the stereotypical messages to your child?

Provocations that challenge or push thinking also arise spontaneously. For instance, in the next story, John talks about inviting an expert on dual-language learning to the center for a family–teacher workshop, to open up thinking on the topic:

When the diversity task force met after the workshop, a couple of teachers commented that they had hoped the speaker would be more explicit about the importance of maintaining home language. I responded that I saw the presenter engaging in a dialogue with family members who had different kinds of language learning situations at home (e.g., only one parent speaks two languages, both parents speak different languages other than English). She provided information about dual-language learning, but also invited family members to problem-solve about what to do in their homes.

Some teachers were in disequilibrium because I was challenging their assumption that we should only be advocating for one approach. I asked the teachers to step back and reflect on the evening as a dialogue between parents who know a great deal about the everyday reality of language learning and professionals who have learned about the importance of supporting home languages. My provocation led to an energizing conversation in which teachers moved out of "we can *teach* families something about this" to "can we create a more authentic *dialogue* in which ideas and experiences are shared?" This approach holds the potential for greater depth in learning and in relationships.

Stakeholder Disagreements. Each of the stakeholders in an early childhood program, including families, staff, and administrators, may have disagreements regarding an anti-bias issue. In many cases, stakeholders remain silent about disagreements, or as in the story from Debbie earlier, wait until leaving the program or much time has passed to share their views and feelings. Both situations make it difficult for the program leader to respond in a collaborative and timely way. Other people may be more explicit and forthcoming with their objections, in which case the leader has an immediate opening for dialogue, depending on the volatility of the disagreement.

Individual personal and cultural histories and an investment in children's well-being are usually the underlying causes. Most likely, the conflict is a resolvable difference in perspective related to issues of equity and bias. It might be the result of a misunderstanding, a lack of information, or a communication breakdown between members of your community.

For instance, a teacher who speaks only English reacts defensively to the program leader's proposal to encourage home languages. She thinks that this will interfere with children's literacy development. Given that the teacher has a professional objection based on misinformation, engaging staff in a workshop on dual-language learning (i.e., providing information) is one route to building the teacher's buy-in.

Disagreements can also occur when there is miscommunication about a program's anti-bias intentions. For instance, an administrator and teacher at a center decided to move forward with using persona dolls in a preschool classroom. Teachers use these dolls to tell stories and engage children in critical thinking and problem solving about a range of cultural and bias issues (Whitney, 2002). Rather than first focusing on the teacher's own classroom, they invited all the center families to a workshop on making dolls and brainstorming ideas for doll identities. The families from the teacher's class had a relationship of trust with her and had already received information about the purpose and use of the dolls. However, families from other classrooms who attended did not understand the rationale for persona dolls and came to voice their concerns. The staff had to backpedal and explain to the family members at the workshop what was the purpose of a persona doll—a very different goal than they had had in mind. While the workshop ended positively by addressing parent concerns, the teachers could have stirred opposition unnecessarily by focusing on the intended outcome and not enough on the steps to get there.

As representatives of a program undergoing change, teachers and administrators are often the targets of disagreements. It is important to realize that parents can also be the ones pushing the change. Disagreements can occur when a parent wants the program to move faster in its anti-bias work than appears to be happening. For example, as John recounts, a parent of color at CSDC questioned why the program had been unsuccessful in hiring teachers of color to reflect the increasing diversity in the families:

Although I agreed that we needed more teachers of color, my first response was to feel defensive. I wanted to justify the situation by explaining the challenges of recruitment in our geographic setting. I also wondered if the parent trusted my commitment. Instead, recognizing my defensiveness, I managed to push it aside, acknowledge that the situation was not satisfactory, and make a verbal commitment to think and act more creatively about ways to bring more ethnic and racial diversity into the adult community at the center. While we continued to be unsuccessful in diversifying the full-time staff, we were able to increase the gender and ethnic/racial diversity among our part-time teachers.

Opposition. When the conflict is opposition, the individual's intent is to stop anti-bias change and question leadership, not to seek a resolution. The intensity of the opposition often indicates the gulf between a stakeholder's views and the anti-bias mission. Again, the personalities and individual histories of those involved can also fuel emotions.

Stakeholders can be very explicit and closed-minded in their objections to anti-bias policies and practices. If someone is simply arguing and not listening, and if emotions are raw, there is not going to be an exchange of viewpoints. This level of conflict can feel uncomfortable and even threatening to those involved, including the program leader.

Returning to the earlier dual-language example, if the underlying reason for the teacher's opposition was her political views regarding the importance of cultural assimilation and learning English in order to be a bona fide "American," she is unlikely to be open to a dialogue about the importance of home language in early learning. In cases such as this, conversations that help the teacher consider her professional responsibility to use what the field considers best practices versus her personal views may lead to her becoming open to trying a dual-language approach. On the other hand, the leader may need to recognize there are limits to change through dialogue and be clear with the teacher about the nonnegotiable values and mission of the program.

Sometimes, opposition to anti-bias values is too great to lead to a solution that works for both parties. A stakeholder may even decide to leave the program if this is a realistic option. When a staff member does not have the option to leave his job, there is still a responsibility to carry out the program's mission—even if he does not agree with all of it. Most parents will also not have the option to leave the program. The best the leader may be able to do is offer and expect a respectful relationship, and make adjustments when possible without abandoning the program's mission.

Opposition may also reflect external political and ideological agendas that reach beyond a program's daily operations. For instance, a political candidate campaigning against immigration reform could zero in on a program's support of dual-language learning. Fortunately, most programs are never embroiled in this kind of public and even hostile opposition to its anti-bias mission and work. We return to this issue at the end of the chapter.

Identity and Emotions

Many stakeholder disagreements are rooted in cultural identity. Essentially, an individual is saying, "this is important to who I am in the world." Understanding the role of identity in disagreements is critical, making it possible to perceive that what appear to be small issues may be rooted in a person's worldview.

When changes challenge cultural values, people's emotions come into play. For some teachers, a shift in the culture of a center—such as changing the holiday policy—may destabilize their sense of belonging. A teacher focused on supporting children to ask questions may feel that her expertise is in doubt when a mother expresses concern that her child shows disrespect to elders by questioning them.

The emotional investment of families connects to their role as the child's ultimate protector. They seek to keep their children safe by ensuring that childrearing choices abide by their cultural norms. For some families, this includes keeping their children safe from bias. For others it can mean keeping them safe from having to talk about, or even experience, difference. For instance, there are very different reactions from parents about the use of persona dolls in the classroom. While one parent may be worried that use of the dolls will raise differences that she believes are (and should be) invisible to her children, another parent may be anxious that a particular doll might be too much like his own child and attract unwanted attention.

BUILDING THE FOUNDATION FOR PRODUCTIVE CONFLICT

As program leader, you have significant influence over the course of anti-bias conflict situations at your program and the potential for positive learning and behavioral outcomes. These efforts do not begin when an angry parent or staff member storms into the office. The program climate you create affects what issues become a conflict, as well as the possibility for productive change through conflict. By *climate*, we mean the emotional tone and quality of interactions between children and adults, including physical proximity, language, and the range of feelings and responses (Greenman, 1995). You should periodically track the climate of the center in relation to the anti-bias mission.

In Chapters 4, 5, and 6, we shared a variety of community-building activities intended to develop teacher and family participation in and commitment to anti-bias education. These activities also create a respectful and warm program climate that helps avoid or de-escalate some potential conflicts. In this section we build on to these activities by considering other strategies and dynamics that are part of a proactive approach to conflict.

Perception and Reality

Uncovering and examining one's own fears about the potential for conflict is an important step. As part of being strategic, it is necessary to think realistically about the possible reactions to anti-bias change from the various stakeholders and broader community. At the same time, you do not want fears about those reactions to rule what you do or do not do. You have to do a mental assessment and determine if your fears stem from a perceived or a real problem. In some cases, a leader's (or teacher's) fears about what *might* happen tap into an internal struggle around a particular issue of diversity and bias. In addition, a lack of knowledge or experience about a specific anti-bias issue can lead to anxiety and uncertainty.

Consider the following examples. A leader sees the need to encourage teachers to be more effective in their inclusion of a child with physical challenges, but is apprehensive about making such a request. She realizes that her own previous difficulties with inclusion as a teacher fuel her fears about how the staff might react. In another situation, a teacher observes that a family from a different cultural group has ideas about toddler dietary needs that differ from his own. He is aware of his lack of information and experience about the family's cultural practices and is worried the parents will be offended if he raises the issue. Finally, a leader and teachers have observed a White child who is exhibiting discriminatory behavior and language toward children of color. The teachers are fearful of how families might respond, and the leader helps them think through a way to approach the issue with tact and clarity.

In these kinds of situations, leaders may find that their fears about how others will respond to anti-bias issues are either unfounded or blown out of proportion. If they act with thoughtful intention and authenticity, leaders will often discover that staff and families are receptive and open to change, even if it takes time.

Institutional Policies as a Starting Place

A core responsibility for any leader is the development of policy that can guide daily practice. From an anti-bias perspective, policies should be the result of a thoughtful and inclusive process removed from specific conflict situations. The intention is to improve clarity and transparency. While policy often has to be responsive to external requirements such as licensing and accreditation, a thoughtful leader can still approach policy development with flexibility, an open mind, and a commitment to an anti-bias approach.

An existing policy can be useful in conflict situations by providing a starting point for thinking about a difference in perspective or even by providing a potential resolution. The leader can reference policies such as ones regarding the inclusion of children of all abilities, the provision of translation services, the program's approach to holidays, and expectations for civil adult behavior.

A program's anti-bias mission statement also provides a reference point for discussing conflicts and searching for solutions. For instance, a family raises concerns about a teacher discussing neighborhood homelessness, which the children observed during a field trip. In response, the program leader can share how the anti-bias mission encourages teachers to be responsive to children's observations of and questions about differences.

Power Dynamics

While the ideal is for all parties in a conflict to enter a discussion as equals, program stakeholders hold different positions of power, formally and informally. As program leader, you hold the most status and power by virtue of your leadership position and responsibilities for supervision, admissions, and policy development. Informal power dynamics also influence relationships. A particular teacher or staff person may hold a higher status than others by virtue of skills, seniority, or ability to influence people. A family member may be able to exercise power by participating on the governing board and committees, by being a spokesperson for other families, or even just by making life unpleasant for staff.

Finding solutions to conflicts can too easily become an issue of who has the power to make a decision. You have the task of leveling out power differences in discussions, so that all participants are part of the problem solving. At the same time, you protect what is nonnegotiable in the program's anti-bias mission; this includes responsibility for identifying what behaviors and practices are and are not acceptable at the center.

If a staff member is being explicitly discriminatory toward children, families, or colleagues, then it becomes a performance and discipline issue. If a family's belief about diversity results in asking for the exclusion of a child, staff, or family member because of that person's identity, then it becomes a breach of the program mission. In those situations, the program leader reinforces the nonnegotiable values and beliefs of the program. We return to this issue later in the chapter.

TURNING CONFLICT INTO GROWTH

Conflict among stakeholders about anti-bias work is not, in principle, about winners and losers. Finding win–win solutions to specific conflicts is always the first strategy. However, reality is likely to be more complex.

We have found that working from the concept of conflict maintenance (Olatunji, 1998) is particularly useful. From this perspective, you manage conflict in a way that moves the program forward to greater equity and inclusion, rather than simply seeking a quick end to the conflict. Managing conflict productively requires dealing with each situation in its real-life context. Listen closely to stakeholders, support the respectful sharing of perspectives, and reflect on decisions in the context of multiple views. This requires perseverance and the ability to accept the uncertainty of not knowing the outcome immediately. It also calls on all involved to be open to changing their thinking and to trying out new ways of acting.

In this section we explore different ways to approach and resolve stakeholder conflicts, including a process we call a third-space solution. We also consider the complexities of anti-bias problem solving and the importance of being clear about the nonnegotiable values in this work.

Find the Third Space

We view the third space as a place where people in conflict, through a distinct process of communication, reach agreement that goes beyond their initial positions. A third-space solution is particularly desirable because it draws on the creativity and openness of both parties to arrive at a new alternative that does not favor either position. This is both an intellectual and emotional experience in which the participants create fresh understandings and solutions. Engaging in it requires that people are willing to enter into dialogue with respect for each other and a willingness to learn (Freire, 1970). When possible, the leader models this process in conflicts with stakeholders and facilitates these discussions between teachers and families.

The following steps of *acknowledge, ask,* and *adapt* constitute a useful third-space strategy for responding to conflicts, particularly those involving differences in cultural perspectives (Derman-Sparks, 2013a).

Step 1: Acknowledge. You, as the leader (or a teacher), acknowledge to yourself that a cultural or values clash exists. You recognize the discomfort and other emotions the parties involved may be feeling and examine your own feelings. You clearly communicate (both verbally and non-verbally) your awareness that a problem exists and needs attending. Do not blame the child or family; the child is often caught in the middle. Perhaps most important, you avoid becoming defensive or making a quick judgment about what underlies the conflict.

Step 2: Ask. You collect information that will contribute to a greater understanding of what underlies the conflict. You talk to the parties involved and to any others you think will provide additional information. Find out what the behavior means to the family, what the family would do in the situation, and what they have done in the past. What is the child's experience at home and at the program? Clarify the priorities in the dilemma and hasten slowly: Do not rush the "ask" step, but keep it timely, because decisions about changes in practice may be necessary.

You also engage in self-reflection, getting clear about your own values and position on the issue causing the conflict and asking, "Do I *want* to make this change?" and if so, "*Can* I make this change?" While a lack of resources, particularly in staffing, is a reality that leaders often have to consider, it can also be a convenient cover for avoiding the complex issues involved in anti-bias conflicts. It is critical to confront doubts and fears about change so that you are honest about your own (and the program's) limitations. Be open to the need for professional growth and expanding your knowledge base as potential elements in a conflict and its resolution.

Step 3: Adapt. You consider ways to adapt policies and practices in your program, taking into account the information gathered in the "acknowledge" and "ask" steps. Find the common ground, and consider alternatives. The objective is to ensure greater responsiveness to cultural practices and alignment with the anti-bias mission. The underlying principle is to find the most effective way to support each child's best growth, taking into account the cultural, diversity, and bias issues in the situation, as well as the needs of all the children and the responsibilities of the program. Adapting is indeed a balancing act. It is also critical to be honest about your nonnegotiable values—what you are and are not willing to change.

Affirm Nonnegotiable Values

Conflict discussions and the resulting outcomes highlight the complexity of anti-bias work. A basic premise is that the anti-bias approach does not mean that all beliefs and values are acceptable. Rather, the four core goals of anti-bias education create a framework within which discussions takes place (Derman-Sparks & Edwards, 2010). In a given situation, one or more anti-bias principles may clash. Since these are not abstract discussions, but attempts to reach behavioral decisions, one principle may have more weight than another may in any given outcome.

Strategic leadership requires you to step back from the fray in order to see what is going on. Both teachers and families can lock into a particular viewpoint about what is best for the child. At times, cultural practices will come into conflict with anti-bias values, and you will need to tread carefully, show sensitivity, and be understanding of how change can be difficult. You have to try to balance the several values of anti-bias education and create movement toward the program's mission. The hope is that ultimately groups in a conflict come together and create a workable solution. Nevertheless, while it is important not to be dogmatic and inflexible about goals, you also do not want to abandon the nonnegotiable values of the program's anti-bias mission.

Sometimes respecting the desires of families, on the one hand, and of practicing nonprejudice and nondiscrimination, on the other hand, may be in contradiction. Consider these possibilities: A parent tells the teacher that he does not want a child with a disability in his son's class because the child will take up too much of the teacher's time. Another parent informs the teacher she does not want her daughter sitting next to a child whose mother is incarcerated. She is afraid that the child will be a bad influence or hurt her own child. Finally, a parent asks the teacher to keep his child out of the dramatic play area because playing there undermines cultural values about the role of men.

How can you balance the principles of respect for a family's beliefs and of nonprejudice and discrimination in these situations? Finding a resolution begins with communicating:

I understand that you are uncomfortable with your child learning about this aspect of diversity. Here at the center we believe strongly that we have to be inclusive of every family. That makes it tough for us to resolve your concern. Tell me more about why you feel so strongly. What might make it more comfortable for you, even though we cannot do what you are asking because it discriminates against other children?

Fortunately, most conflict situations that rest on cultural differences in childrearing practices have reachable solutions. All parties usually have to accept some changes from what they had wanted. Sometimes the balance tips in favor of the family's needs, at other times in favor of the program. In some cases, you would need to make a final decision, especially when the issue concerns what happens at the program or affects the community rather than a single family or staff member. If it is about a practice at the center, you may need to say, "Well, this is the best we can do," and the parent may respond, "Okay, we can live with that." If it is a practice in the home, ultimately the parents have the right to make that decision if it does not affect what happens in the program.

You will also have times when you have to let go of a desired outcome, at least for the time being, in order to build deeper relationships of trust in the program. We have found that even when a third-space outcome is not possible, staff, families, and administrators still learn from the exploration of the multiple perspectives about the specific conflict. Deeper and more authentic relationships often result.

Recognize Agreeable Solutions for Differing Conflicts

Each conflict solution is unique to the situation under consideration. While the third-space procedure of "acknowledge, ask, and adapt" works for different kinds of conflict, there are no one-size-fits-all outcomes. The purpose of the "acknowledge, ask, and adapt" procedure is to help people generate a solution that best fits the context of their conflict.

Several types of other outcomes are also possible and acceptable, including the following:

1. The program leader or teacher understands and agrees to follow the solution preferred by the family member to maintain consistency with the family's childrearing beliefs.
2. The family and program leader and/or teacher agree to an action that is a modification of what each of them does.

3. The family, upon understanding why a program or teacher uses a particular practice, approves the practice or decides to live with it. (Derman-Sparks, 2013a)

The following examples, adapted from our collective experiences, illustrate different conflict situations: between a family and the program; between staff members; between a staff member and the program leader. Our intention is to give you a sense of what they look like, with the caveat that each process is unique.

Who Diapers? A family brought to the program leader their concerns about a male caregiver diapering their daughter. Their unease reflected their cultural values and views about child development, which were in conflict with the program's ethical values concerning the importance and rights of men as caregivers. Early conversations with the parents focused on assuring them that the staff had heard their concerns and viewed them as important. As the staff moved into the "ask" stage, it became apparent that many of the parents' concerns had a lot to do with their own process of coming to terms with developmental changes in their daughter as she moved out of toddlerhood. The teachers thoughtfully considered the various issues in the conflict.

Although wanting to respect cultural and family issues, the program leader realized that the rights of the male teacher were equally important to consider. There were several possible solutions, but none might be able to meet everyone's needs. How should the program adapt? Meeting the family's expressed needs meant assuring them that only female caregivers would do the diapering. However, the staff and program leader agreed that this solution violated their professional code of ethics opposing gender discrimination, and that their ethical responsibility to the male caregiver was paramount. Essentially, they said to the family, "We understand why you are uncomfortable, but we cannot exclude the male caregiver from this task. It would unfairly imply that he was not able to safely carry out a basic responsibility as a teacher of infants and toddlers."

At the same time, the program leader offered to develop a written policy about diapering of children. This policy addressed some of the parents' issues concerning safety and supervision, and applied to both male and female caregivers. The family was satisfied with this solution, so ultimately, the program was able to come to an agreeable third-space resolution, and avoid moving into an oppositional response. The family learned about the importance of male caregivers in infant/toddler classrooms; the program leader and staff gained a deeper appreciation of the gender issues families face negotiating in unfamiliar cultural terrain, and the program gained new and useful policies.

Are the Holiday Decorations Appropriate? Teachers have varying levels of under-standing of anti-bias issues that raise the possibility of conflicts and the search for a third-space solution. John talks about his experience with the difficult issue of holiday celebrations:

When I arrived at CSDC, a tradition existed of arranging items at the front entrance to represent the changing seasons. For winter, there were ski boots and skis, but also some items such as colored lights, wreaths, and other decorations associated with Christmas—although nothing as obvious as a Santa Claus or nativity scene. Shortly after we shared our new diversity mission statement with the families, a parent sent me an email objecting to the decorations in her child's classroom and at the entrance as symbols of Christmas time. She explicitly referenced our diversity mission statement, essentially holding us accountable to it.

I shared the email with the teachers and asked them to reflect on how the current practice fits with our diversity mission. Some teachers interpreted the parent's objec-tions as an attack on their identity, insisting, "Now we can never talk about Christmas." My response was, "Let's talk about that. Let's look at our reactions and think about what the parent is requesting."

After considerable discussion, we decided that the existing policy on holiday cel-ebrations did not address the complexity of the issue. Together, we created a set of values to accompany our existing holiday policy [Child Study and Development Center, 2013]. This provided us with guidelines to address conflicting desires around holidays in the program. The guidelines, in themselves, reflect the multiple issues that a pro-gram must take into account, as the following three illustrate:

- We believe that each family reflects larger cultural practices and values in their own unique ways as "home culture." Families (and children) should take the initiative in sharing home culture in the classroom.
- We realize that teachers hold a position of power/authority in the classroom community and need to be mindful *not* to present or initiate discussions and activities related to religion or culture that could exclude or offend families.
- We are conscious that we must consider the pervasiveness of dominant (ma-jority) religious and cultural practices and values in our community and seek to ensure that *all* families feel included at the center.

While some teachers may have felt constrained by the policy, the teaching staff as a whole saw the new values as a tool for balancing several needs within any given group of families.

Cleanliness or Creativity? Some of the families complained to the program leader that their children came home with their clothes covered in paint. They want to find a way to keep the clothing clean or to eliminate easel painting. With careful listening, the leader uncovered two core issues: First, some par-ents are concerned that the neighborhood views their children negatively be-cause they look messy; and second, parents who use a laundromat are feeling overwhelmed by the extra washing. At a staff meeting, some teachers suggested using smocks that covered the children entirely. Others objected, arguing that having to stop for smocks might interfere with a child's creativity. Finally, they agreed that paying attention to the negative impact on families (especially those without washing machines) was as important as spontaneous creativity. The center purchased a large supply of second-hand men's shirts to use as smocks. Easel painting did not diminish, but paint on clothes did. Everyone was satisfied.

Is It Professional? In this example, two beliefs about being an effective teacher come into conflict. One is the premise that the professional role of the teacher requires a separation between one's personal (home) and professional (work) lives in order to maintain objectivity in relationships with children and families (L.G. Katz, 1985). The second is the anti-bias principle about the importance of being aware of your own social and cultural identities and sharing your understanding of them with colleagues and families.

Some teachers at the center were uncomfortable with the way that other colleagues talked about their social-class identity with families. Those who did share often identified as working class and argued that it helped with making social class visible in the center, building authentic relationships, and supporting families with similar circumstances.

In response to the conflict, the program leader called a staff meeting on the topic and commented that, while the program needs boundaries regarding what staff share about their personal lives with families, boundary rules also may keep some identity differences invisible. The staff then discussed the questions: Are there differences in sharing your personal identity with families (our clients) and teachers (our colleagues)? How can we talk about social class and still maintain our view of professionalism? The leader also referenced the issues raised by the *Code of Ethical Conduct and Statement of Commitment* (NAEYC, 2011), which advises against personal relationships with families that might be exploitive or weaken a teacher's effectiveness.

While the discussions did not create an end point in the conflict, they did serve to open up the issue to thoughtful reflection about identity and invisibility. The leader had to take responsibility for drawing some boundaries about sharing personal information, while also realizing that anti-bias conflicts have many gray areas that need to be revisited and grappled with over time.

Winter Clothing Swap. At times, the program leader and teachers develop a third-space solution in response to an anti-bias need that does not involve an explicit conflict between specific individuals. John describes an example at CSDC:

As part of an ongoing discussion about the role of social–economic class issues at the center, I asked the teachers to think about ways in which we implicitly expected families to have access to material resources. One issue that arose was the financial stresses for some families regarding our requirement for additional clothing items that permitted outdoor play in all kinds of weather (e.g., additional mittens, boots, and indoor slippers). We brainstormed a set of recommendations about ways to make additional clothing items available at the center without putting the spotlight on families with fewer resources. Working with the Parent Advisory Committee, we decided on an annual winter clothing exchange in which families brought in unneeded children's winter gear and took home clothing they needed. The parent advisory committee organized the clothing swap, and most families participated. Left-over items were donated to a local shelter.

Professional Ethics vs. Personal Beliefs. During a schoolwide theme about families, one teacher objected to talking with children about gay and lesbian families, because of religious beliefs. Another worried that some families might also oppose any mention of same-sex families. With the leader's facilitation, the staff considered the issue in light of their anti-bias values and goals. In the end, the teachers affirmed that being inclusive was the priority: "We seek a community where every family and child has a right to be visible in the classroom. Someone else's beliefs shouldn't make another person feel invisible." The program leader also helped the teachers develop clear language they could use to explain the purpose of the curriculum theme to families.

Based on the program's anti-bias mission and the ECCE professional ethic of serving *all* children and their families, inclusiveness trumps the teacher's personal belief. While program leaders can provide professional development that exposes staff to different ideas, they cannot tell someone what to believe. Drawing on their identity as professionals, teachers can often find a way to move forward and live with the contradiction between a personal belief and the program's anti-bias values.

Maintain the Values Basis of Anti-Bias Education

Leaders need to be prepared for the misconception that anti-bias education means all beliefs and actions are acceptable. This oppositional strategy can get very confusing for a leader who is also committed to creating a democratic and caring community. Parents or staff may use the argument "We thought you appreciated all beliefs here" as a way to defend practices that conflict with anti-bias values.

Practices that stereotype or discriminate against individuals because of their membership in particular groups are never acceptable in an anti-bias approach. Consider the following example: A teacher tends to direct girls to playing house and dress up and discourages active, running-around games outside, while she directs boys to blocks and trucks and discourages them from dressing up in the dramatic play area and encourages them to play active games outside. The teacher regularly praises boys for their intelligence and girls for looking pretty. The program leader intervenes, explaining to the teacher that differential treatment of boys and girls is discriminatory and hurtful to their development. The teacher counters that the leader is not allowing her to practice her beliefs, so the program is hypocritical about its anti-bias mission.

Even in these kinds of conflicts, trying to use the "acknowledge, ask, and adapt" process is still the place to begin. The approach is, "Let's talk about what it means to be able to include and serve all families at this program and make this as inclusive as possible." As mentioned previously, the leader needs to enter these conversations with clarity and confidence about nonnegotiable anti-bias values. On occasions, it may become clear that the conflict is really a case of opposition and resistance to anti-bias education.

RESPONDING TO OPPOSITION

As long as people are open to finding solutions, including living with a contradiction between a personal belief and a professional anti-bias value, then a program moves forward. Sometimes, however, a program stakeholder opposes or resists a part of or the entire anti-bias education approach. In these cases, the person (or group) usually does not want to enter into a dialogue, but rather to obstruct or end anti-bias efforts. A stakeholder who takes this oppositional stance may try to get other stakeholders and outside people to join in the stand against the program.

Be Strategic

When you think and act strategically in response to conflict of this kind, it is manageable, even if it is also unpleasant. On the other hand, a hasty reaction can undermine a program's work. It is essential to stay calm and not take these attacks personally. Opposition can be destructive to anti-bias education efforts if you are not self-aware or clear about goals or do not have a range of potential strategies in your repertoire.

If needed, you can intentionally deflect some of the emotional heat away from staff so they can continue their work in the classroom. Teachers are involved in a close relationship with parents—they are helping to care for their children—which means there is a lot of emotional vulnerability. You are in the best position to deal with the emotions that come with opposition. If the parent is annoyed with you, the conflict has less affect on the teacher's ability to work with the child and family.

In the following example, a parent came to the program leader to criticize the quality of the children's books in a classroom. As the leader listened carefully and tried to find out more about the specifics of what the parent did not like, it seemed that the "quality" issue was a screen for something else—opposition to the inclusion of children's books with gay and lesbian families. Rather than circling around the problem, the leader then tried to establish that they needed to be honest with each other if they were going to have a useful discussion. Naming the conflict explicitly, the leader tried to establish a third-space dialogue. The parent angrily denied this and began questioning the leader's competency.

In this situation it became clear to the program leader that the goal of the parent was to obstruct movement toward the program's anti-bias mission, not to engage in dialogue and problem solving. The parent later went to a meeting of the center's parent committee to question the anti-bias mission and the "out-of-date" children's literature. After a discussion, the committee, whose members had participated in learning about anti-bias education, backed the anti-bias mission and the leader's commitment.

Unable to stop the center's anti-bias mission, the parent unsuccessfully attempted to discredit the leader's reputation in the larger professional community. Early childhood leaders can feel professionally vulnerable due to their complex responsibilities and accountability to licensing, accreditation, and numerous clients. Fortunately, the leader was an active member of local and state professional organizations and had built a network of allies in anti-bias work. Their emotional support and advice was a reminder that there are colleagues out there who would deal with the opposition in a similar way. The leader also appraised the child-care licensor of the situation.

While the leader had to spend unwelcome time and energy on dealing with this situation and lost some sleep, it ended without any negative impact on the program and its anti-bias work. The conflict also became an opportunity to affirm the program's commitment to anti-bias values and to be more visible about its efforts. Upon reflection, the leader realized that the groundwork done over the course of several years had resulted in critical support during this public visibility of anti-bias values.

External Opposition

More rarely, opposition and even attacks may come from political organizations external to the program that oppose all forms of multicultural, anti-bias, and social justice education. They put forward moral, religious, and patriotic objections such as not celebrating Christmas as everyone's holiday is anti-Christian and bilingual programs are anti-American. These groups also focus on issues especially relevant to the ECCE field. This may include decrying the effect of children's rights on family authority and complaining that ECCE teachers are not competent in preparing children for later schooling.

Typically, these oppositional groups are not interested in dialogue or negotiation with the groups or individuals they attack. Instead, they attempt to stir up and exploit controversy around a program's anti-bias work for their political and social agenda. In most situations, external attacks on a particular program go away, and these groups move on to the next controversy that will draw media and supporter attention to their cause.

Here is an example of how a Head Start program dealt with hostile and public opposition from an outside group. Again, it is an issue of children's books depicting gay and lesbian families in the story and images.

A regional Head Start agency held a workshop for its staff about selecting children's books, which included displays of books for multicultural education. A parent from one of the agency's centers who attended the workshop became very upset by the inclusion of stories with gay and lesbian families and contacted a political advocacy group in which she participated. The group mounted a campaign against the regional agency that had presented the workshop, claiming that the entire national Head Start program was teaching children to be homosexual. The agency countered this attack by inviting the media to visit the area's Head Start centers to observe teachers working with children and to talk with staff about the purpose of including children's books depicting a range of people and families. In addition, agency staff disseminated information about national Head Start's commitment to diversity, to the media, early childhood organizations, and community organizations in the agency's region. In the end, the larger community came to the program's support, and the campaign against them dissipated. More people were now aware of and better informed about Head Start's work.

When faced with opposition from an outside political group it is essential that you take a deep breath, stay calm, and recognize that you need allies to help you deal with the situation. You must be clear and articulate about the rationale for anti-bias education and draw on the program's reputation and community support. It is also important to be wary about wasting time and resources trying to convince such groups about the value of anti-bias education or to try to come to a negotiated solution. In the end, you need to keep your focus on the stakeholders the program serves.

THOUGHTFUL RISK TAKING

The early childhood leader constantly assesses what needs to change, what can change, and how teachers and families will embrace and engage in making change that is lasting and significant. To use conflict productively as part of the change process, the leader takes a long-term view. This means being proactive instead of reactive, picking one's battles, and prioritizing where to invest energy and resources.

From a strategic point of view, a leader faced with difficult anti-bias conflicts sometimes needs to ask: "How willing am I to put myself on the line and put my position in jeopardy? Are there limits to the ways I would temper my anti-bias commitment?" These are very personal questions. To answer them, individuals bring their own complexities to deal with, including their identity, learning style, and life history. Each leader has a certain comfort level with disagreement and heated discussion, and both dispositions and vulnerabilities with regard to taking risks. As a woman of Asian descent, Debbie points out that she is sensitive to staff or families accusing her of advocating for an anti-bias agenda simply because she is Chinese American:

I have had to figure out when to push and when to hold back because of these per-ceptions. I walk a fine line. I also did not want teachers to view me as the expert on Chinese New Year or Chinese culture. While I am willing to share my knowledge, I risk having my cultural identity trivialized or pigeonholed. When a teacher suggested a schoolwide Chinese New Year celebration, I suggested we change it to a "New Year celebration" and explore all the different ways cultures represented in the school cel-ebrated—Lunar New Year, Jewish New Year, Russian New Year, Greek New Year, and so on. This allowed children, families, and staff to compare and contrast the different rituals and traditions.

A leader moving into a new center has to be strategic about building sup-port and allies before "pushing too many buttons." That is sensible. Regard-less of commitment and passion to an anti-bias approach, it simply is not wise for a leader to come in the first day and send out a newsletter that changes a long-held tradition even if it violates an anti-bias value. Becoming a lightning rod for everyone's fears and ignorance is not likely to serve a leader's goals.

Whenever conflict about an anti-bias issue unexpectedly flares up, it is easy to feel stress because you do not know where the conflict is going to lead. These realities underline the importance of understanding the role of conflict and disequilibrium in movement toward your anti-bias mission and the signif-icance of thinking and acting proactively to create a positive role for conflict. Conflict is one indicator that movement is happening; the program culture is shifting toward greater equity and inclusion. When stakeholders are not ques-tioning the way things are, or having a disagreement over policy or practice around diversity, you should wonder if the program is settling into a comfort-able place, rather than moving forward on its anti-bias mission.

You have to be comfortable with and confident about the decisions you make and actions you take regarding conflict. Someone else who is equally committed to anti-bias values might come to a different solution or decision. You may even come to think of a "better" strategy in hindsight. There is no perfect solution for any given conflict situation, just one that makes the best sense in that particular context. Part of the trick is living with some ambiguity in these situations and moving forward.

In the next chapter we build on the process of "reading" your program discussed in Chapter 3 by turning to the program leader's ongoing work of documenting anti-bias change as the basis for setting future goals and strategy.

CHAPTER 8

Documenting the Shift Toward Anti-Bias Change

Documenting our anti-bias work forced me to articulate my thoughts and questions and pushed me to reflect more deeply. It was also a way to share with the larger community what we were doing and get their feedback too.

—Teacher

Documenting changes in the culture of a program is a challenging but necessary leadership role. Program leaders have an ethical responsibility to hold themselves accountable to move forward in their anti-bias mission.

Documentation is the process of observing and recording in order to make the dynamics and content of change more visible. Engaging in this process enables you to make sense of it, to learn from it, to share it with others, and to determine next steps in your work. Krechevsky, Rivard, and Burton (2010) view "documentation as a powerful tool for supporting three forms of accountability: (a) accountability to self, (b) accountability to each other, and (c) accountability to the larger community" (p. 65). Systematic documentation provides the information needed to assess your effectiveness in meeting goals and objectives and then setting new ones.

Documenting change in a program's culture, children, staff, and leader throughout the year guides the forward movement of anti-bias work. You can identify accomplishments, what more needs doing, and the patterns of change in your program at the individual, classroom, and program levels. Revisions in practice and policy; transformations in beliefs, assumptions, and attitudes; and shifts in the relationships among community members are all part of what gets documented and analyzed.

This chapter begins with a discussion of the complexity of change, a perspective that guides our thinking about documentation in an anti-bias approach. We then propose indicators to look for in the following areas: (1) the leader's growth and efficacy; (2) teachers' growth in anti-bias classroom practice, awareness, and related dispositions and skills; (3) children's progress in meeting anti-bias goals; and (4) the shifts in the broader program culture, including families, policy, environments, and networks. We also offer some tools that leaders can use in documenting all these areas of growth and change.

RECOGNIZING THE COMPLEXITY OF CHANGE

The passage of change can be subtle, abrupt, slow, and dynamic. We emphasize the complex, systemic, and incremental nature of the change process that program leaders are trying to track and from which they seek to learn. As we have emphasized throughout this book, anti-bias education change is a journey, rather than a set of products or finite outcomes at the end of a linear trajectory. The multiple layers of change for the leader, children, families, teachers, and program are interrelated and often difficult to untangle and measure. Because an ECCE program is a system of relationships, you can never be certain how, when, and in what ways your efforts affect the thinking and actions of others. For instance, when you observe a teacher introducing a new learning experience on exploring hair texture with children, is it a result of various conversations and workshops you have initiated, or is it the result of the teacher's own journey of discovery? Or both?

One of the key challenges for you is capturing the changes in a staff's consciousness as well as the quality of adult–child and adult–adult interactions and relationships. The authenticity and effectiveness of an anti-bias program is as much a function of these elements as it is a result of changes in the curriculum and learning materials. Yet how can warmth, authenticity, fairness, and productive conflict in human relationships be documented?

Although documenting changes in consciousness and interactions is delicate, it is important to try. We therefore suggest a set of criteria or markers for the program leader and staff as the basis for documentation and reflection. We drew on the broad goals for children and anti-bias educators outlined in Chapter 1 as the primary source for developing criteria relevant to the work of program leaders and staff.

Documentation is not only about capturing forward movement toward your anti-bias mission. Inevitably, this work includes times when the program seems to be in a holding pattern. At other times, it seems like change is regressing. These are also occasions for careful documentation and reflection. Are there other demands (like preparing for licensing) that are sapping energy? Have you intentionally decided to back off on challenging teachers because they feel stressed due to upcoming parent–teacher conferences? It is important to understand and be intentional about the pace and direction of your anti-bias efforts.

Lastly, the information and analysis of the initial "reading" of the program (see Chapter 3) becomes a baseline for documenting and reflecting on what is changing, what is not changing, and the patterns of change. For instance, knowing whether a program has a history of reflective practice or encouraging productive conflict will be important in later considering the depth of the teachers' dialogue about identity and bias. The initial reading of a program helps determine how and what to document in a particular setting.

DOCUMENTING PROGRAM LEADER GROWTH AND EFFICACY

In anti-bias work, you start with yourself. Even if you knew this when you undertook the journey, taking the time to reflect on your growth periodically, as an anti-bias leader, is easy to neglect. Your focus is on the change happening for teachers and families, and there are the demands of everyday administrative and supervisory responsibilities to draw your attention away from anti-bias goals.

In this section we propose indicators of change in your work as a leader to use in your self-reflection process and offer some strategies and tools for documenting and making sense of these changes.

Indicators of Leader Change

The first set of indicators emphasizes the foundational work of learning about social identity and the dynamics and history of oppression and activism. We follow this with indicators of a range of skills and dispositions relevant to anti-bias leadership. *Dispositions* are enduring habits of mind that affect how children and adults approach and respond to everyday interactions and tasks (Carter & Curtis, 1994; L. G. Katz, 1993).

To help illustrate these indicators, we provide examples of how some of these changes could look in practice. It is also useful to refer back to the initial reading of leader readiness for anti-bias work as the baseline from which change occurred (see Chapter 3).

Self-Awareness and Knowledge. Are you

- Developing your awareness and understanding of, and ability to share, your social identity?
- Examining and sharing what you have learned about human differences and connection?
- Identifying how institutional "isms" advantage or disadvantage you and the stereotypes and prejudices you hold about yourself or others?
- Exploring your ideas, feelings, and experiences of social justice activism?

Leadership Skills and Dispositions. Are you

- Integrating anti-bias change into all aspects of your role as a leader and the workings of the program, rather than seeing it as a narrow or separate focus?
- Feeling more at ease with and valuing disequilibrium as part of your anti-bias efforts?
- Taking a long-term and strategic view of your anti-bias efforts balanced with the urgency of social justice?

- Growing more comfortable and strategic in your approach to conflicts with various stakeholders?
- Becoming more articulate and clear in communicating the purpose and rationale for your anti-bias mission in your interaction with others? For instance, you decide to share an overview of the anti-bias mission during your admissions tours with families.
- Demonstrating clarity and awareness of your ethical boundaries regarding anti-bias work (your nonnegotiables)? For instance, when a staff member raises objections to having a poster of same-sex families on the wall, you calmly explain the importance of making all families feel included in the community.
- Developing your ability to recognize and be at ease with the gray areas (complexity and ambiguity) in anti-bias work?
- Becoming more skillful in negotiating and finding the third space in resolving conflicts with stakeholders?
- Making efforts to share and advocate for your anti-bias approach more visibly in your work outside of the program?

Tools for Documenting Growth and Efficacy as a Leader

Examining your own effectiveness as an anti-bias education leader is a tricky process, fraught with your own subjectivity. You are your best and worst critic. At times, you will be overly hard on yourself and find little to celebrate. At other times, you will be unaware of the missteps you have taken or the opportunities you have missed.

The Internal Process. Take the time to document your thoughts, feelings, and actions through regular journaling in whatever ways work for you (e.g., writing in a book or on a computer, recording your self-reflections orally on tape or into your computer). Having a written or aural record is important to being able to revisit your journey over time. You can also engage in a more systematic approach by using a formal tool such as the Self-Study Guide presented in the next section on teacher change (Chen et al., 2009). Although the authors designed this tool for classroom teachers, the sections on "raising self-awareness" and "relationships with families and community" dovetail with the indicators of leader change noted earlier.

Turning to Colleagues. Leaders also need to reach outside of themselves to assess their growth and effectiveness. Sharing your thinking, concerns, and successes with trusted colleagues and allies on a regular basis (e.g., by email or at support meetings) provides you with a significant window into how you are doing. Visiting colleagues' programs is another way to become more aware of your own work. For example, John notes:

I observed the way in which Debbie's program had effectively supported the full inclusion of children with special needs. After talking with her, I realized the need to be more proactive in using my budget creatively to ensure teachers had the capacity and resources to support all children.

Trusted colleagues and other allies in the community have the advantage of not being one's supervisor, with whom you might not want to discuss some issues about your personal development. Similarly, some aspects of your thinking and decision-making process are not appropriate to share with teachers and families because they may lead to misunderstanding and a loss of trust.

Feedback from Stakeholders. Reaching out to the program's primary stakeholders for specific feedback about one's anti-bias leadership is also essential. Families and staff see your work from very different perspectives than colleagues and allies—or supervisors—do. You can seek feedback more formally through surveys or in more intimate settings, such as a staff anti-bias or diversity task force or a family advisory group. Unlike surveys, which are typically anonymous and one-way, these meetings can provide you with more specific and detailed feedback from stakeholders who share your commitment to the ABE mission. Remember, as program leader you hold a position of power over teachers and families. The atmosphere of trust and openness that exists within these groups will partly determine the authenticity of the feedback.

Despite their limitations, surveys do provide a broad take on how stakeholders view your effectiveness, with a continuum from avid supporters of your anti-bias efforts through to folks who misunderstand and/or even detest your commitment. We discuss the annual survey as a source of feedback later in this chapter. Program leaders can also seek out feedback from staff through a more anonymous survey process (including the use of free online survey tools) for the entire staff or through a more lengthy written or verbal feedback process with teachers involved in leadership of anti-bias efforts. A staff survey could include a very broad question such as *How effective is the director [or whatever term a program prefers] in developing and promoting a clear anti-bias vision and mission for the center?*

Debbie began an open and very collegial dialogue with her lead teachers using the questions: What does a leader need to do to create an anti-bias education atmosphere? What do you as teachers need from the program leader? John used the same questions with teachers in his program's diversity/ABE taskforce as part of a written format. We have excerpted some of these responses as "teacher" quotes throughout this book.

DOCUMENTING CHANGE IN TEACHERS AND IN THEIR CLASSROOMS

Teachers are at the core of implementing the anti-bias approach in the classroom for the most important stakeholders—the children. As coach, mentor, and supervisor, you have a key vantage point from which to document and review teacher change and their implementation of anti-bias education at the ground level.

We begin with a description of indicators of teachers' classroom practice and then describe attitudes and behaviors (i.e., dispositions and skills) that reflect essential, although less tangible, ways of interacting with colleagues and families. We have found that leaders and teachers often overlook these indicators, which reflect the anti-bias educator goals shared in Chapter 1. They are critical to the depth and authenticity of anti-bias education and affirm the teacher's role beyond the classroom. We then turn to some strategies and tools for documenting these changes.

Indicators of Teacher Change in the Classroom

Teacher anti-bias education change and efficacy is most visible in the classroom. A good deal of your documentation comes from what you observe in the process of coaching, mentoring, and supervising teachers in their direct work with children and families (see Chapter 6).

Classroom Practice. This section puts the spotlight on what teachers do in their classrooms. It suggests broad indicators that reflect the four anti-bias education goals in practice with the children. Look for the interactions and facilitating that teachers offer to the children during activities, as well as the specific activities. It is also useful to document teachers' handling of teachable moments that arise.

Do teachers:

- Regularly initiate activities that foster children's awareness and appreciation of all aspects of their personal and social identities? For instance, the teachers help children explore personal and social identities throughout the subject themes (e.g., learning about myself) and subject domains (e.g., art, science). They regularly notice and actively pick up on teachable moments when children's conversation and play reflect their curiosity, ideas, and attitudes about themselves.
- Regularly initiate activities that promote children's learning and appreciation of human differences and similarities among people (identity and culture) and actively integrate this topic into other content themes and learning domains?

- Notice and actively pick up on teachable moments and emergent curriculum when children's conversation, questions, and play reflect their curiosity, ideas, and attitudes about human differences and similarities? For instance, when a child makes a comment about a Native American dad's long hair braid, the teacher affirms the observation and later implements a curriculum to explore diversity in men's hair styles using picture books and photographs.
- Create a classroom environment that reflects the families and community in authentic ways and implement a curriculum that draws from the social identities, culture, and ecologies of the children and families?
- Demonstrate warmth, equity, and cultural responsiveness in interactions with children and families?
- Model clear and appropriate language for talking about difference, similarity, bias, and equity?
- Intervene whenever a child makes prejudiced or discriminatory comments to another child, make clear that such behavior is not acceptable, and help children work through the situation? (See Derman-Sparks & Edwards, 2010; Ramsey, 2004.)
- Guide children in engaging in activism in their school and community in meaningful ways? (See Derman-Sparks & Edwards, 2010; Pelo & Davidson, 2000.) For instance, the children notice that the languages of some families are not included on the signs outside the center and work with teachers and families to create signs.

Teacher Awareness and Related Dispositions and Skills. We now turn to indicators of change in the less tangible aspects of anti-bias change—teachers' anti-bias awareness and related dispositions and skills. The developmental framework for the adult anti-bias journey (presented in Chapter 1, and in an abridged format in Chapter 3) provides a more detailed way of looking at growth in a teacher's anti-bias awareness. We view this framework as a helpful tool for informing a leader's interactions with staff (and families), but as too complex for ongoing documentation of teachers. The indicators below are a list of behaviors that you can look for throughout the year and can use in figuring out how to scaffold teacher growth and plan appropriate professional development opportunities.

As with all anti-bias change, these attitudes and behaviors will show times of forward progress *and* backward movement. Noticing when teachers may be resistant, feel frustration or discomfort, or demonstrate a lack of skill or knowledge, is as necessary as paying attention to their growth. These times are often a part of the process of long-term growth and change. Documentation also helps you identify and tease out the dynamics of teachers who remain "silent" or peripheral participants in anti-bias work. Is this a reflection of personal style, or comfort level, or trust? You need to pay attention to what you do not hear, as well as what you do.

Look for indicators of growth in anti-bias consciousness and actions. Do teachers:

- Show willingness and greater ease with asking questions about anti-bias education?
- Seek out the program leader and collegial support in problem-solving anti-bias issues?
- Participate more actively in conversations about anti-bias issues, demonstrate greater open-mindedness and willingness to change their thinking because of new information, and expanded perspectives? For instance, they show greater acceptance of the complexity and disequilibrium in dealing with anti-bias issues, including not knowing.
- Identify and relate observations of social identity development and bias in interactions with other adults and in the program?
- Demonstrate willingness to share aspects of one's social identity with colleagues and families, while maintaining appropriate professional boundaries? For instance, a teacher tells parents and children (few of whom are Jewish) that she will be away in order to observe Yom Kippur and shares what she will be doing.
- Engage in anti-bias self-reflection and learning (e.g., reading books), and take the initiative in this process? For instance, a teacher shares that she has been reading the book *Nickel and Dimed* (Ehrenreich, 2011) to deepen her understanding of the lives of some of her families.
- Demonstrate movement beyond their comfort zones by taking thoughtful risks in the classroom with new activities and strategies for the anti-bias curriculum and in work with families?
- Show growth in their ability to work through third-space solutions with families and colleagues in anti-bias conflicts?
- Communicate anti-bias values, information, and intention to families and colleagues using different formats? For instance, a teacher shares the developmental rationale for ABE goals for children as part of a parent–teacher conference.
- Take a leadership role in anti-bias initiatives at the center? For instance, a teacher introduces the program leader to the director of a nearby Latino cultural center and proposes they hold the staff retreat there.

Processes and Tools for Documenting Teacher Change

Documentation of teacher change occurs in three core ways:

- The leader's ongoing observation of teachers as the basis for scaffolding their growth

- The teachers' self-study process
- The leader's supervision and assessment of teacher performance

Each of these processes overlaps at various points. For instance, your ongoing observation and the teacher's self-study may be included as part of a teacher's annual performance assessment. Likewise, you can use the teacher goals negotiated as part of the annual assessment to guide teacher self-study or ongoing coaching and mentorship.

Ongoing Observation. You observe teachers at work in the classroom and in other contexts such as informal conversations, individual and group meetings, and in staff trainings. Using the indicators of teacher change as a guide, you can document teacher anti-bias competencies through various documentation media, including written (e.g., anecdotal observations or checklists) and visual/auditory (e.g., photographic, video, audio recordings). In making use of these documentation opportunities, you need to be observant, organized, and intentional.

Teacher Self-Study Tool. In collaboration with Dora Chen and Heather Fraser, John helped to develop the "Self-Study Guide for Reflecting on Anti-Bias Curriculum Planning and Implementation," a tool to assist teachers in studying their anti-bias development and practice in a systematic and intentional way (Chen et al., 2009; see Appendix B online at www.tcpress.com). You can also use this tool to work with each teacher in reflecting on growth and setting new goals.

Using the Self-Study Guide, teachers record at regular intervals examples of practice that reflect their growth and challenges in the four key domains. Each domain includes a set of specific questions intended to prompt teacher reflection:

A. Raising self-awareness (e.g., "Am I aware of my own cultural identity and history?")
B. Physical environment (e.g., "Do all children have equal opportunity to participate in activities?")
C. Pedagogical environment (e.g., "Are my verbal and nonverbal messages free of stereotypes and hidden biases?")
D. Relationships with families and community (e.g., "Do I have enough knowledge of the local community to extend children's learning beyond the classroom walls?"). (Excerpted from Chen et al., 2009, pp. 105–106)

In designing the tool, John and his colleagues assumed that anti-bias change is a very personal and often uncomfortable process. "Our goal was to create a tool that invited a personal and introspective level of reflection, educated the user, and encouraged incremental changes in practice over time"

(Chen et al., 2009, p. 104). Of particular note, they structured the tool to reflect a developmental progression in how a teacher views her own growth from "This is new territory for me" to "I do this with ease" and from more internal processes to more public practice.

We see the tool being useful for both individual and collaborative reflection by educators but are cautious about viewing it as a format for external assessment. The program leader or an experienced teacher can also use the tool as part of a mentoring relationship with a teacher who is new to anti-bias education. One of the interesting dynamics about self-study on anti-bias change is that individuals tend to be more critical of their awareness, skills, and knowledge as they move further along in the anti-bias journey. "Using the tool is a necessarily *subjective* process in which one's responses will undoubtedly be impacted by what one knows about oneself (self-awareness), how honest one is prepared to be, and one's internalized values regarding diversity" (Chen et al., 2009, p. 104).

The following story from a teacher highlights that critical self-reflection also emerges spontaneously in response to particular activities the teacher does with her children. These moments also provide valuable evidence of growth. In this case, the teacher has been actively involved for some years in an anti-bias journey. Her story reveals a willingness to scrutinize her own reactions in an honest and very public way, which would not be possible for a teacher new to anti-bias education.

I had chosen a book to read [in my class] at meeting [that] talks about the change in seasons and which tied in perfectly to the curriculum in the classroom and the observations children were having. It seemed fairly benign, but as soon as I began to read it in the context of my classroom, I felt this awful pit in my stomach [as the story talks about the brown landscape]. Then it hits me; depending on how this is read or interpreted, children could think that brown is bad. At that moment, a child in my room proudly shouted, "Hey [Teacher]! I have brown skin!" I thought to myself, "You have got to take this on . . . how do I react. The . . . [child] is watching. My reaction to this book and the child's statement will speak volumes." And then I spoke: "You are right. You have beautiful brown skin. And you know what? When I see the brown grass and the brown soil, I get really excited [because] I know that means that the snow has melted and that spring is on its way."

We had a team meeting the next day, and I revealed the second-guessing, the embarrassment, and struggles I felt. All of the things I felt inside were unnoticeable by the adults around me. . . . I think part of my reason for sharing it was to talk myself through what had happened but also because it was a teachable moment for me, my team, and our students. Diversity work is never finished for me—it is an ongoing, self-reflective journey.

Annual Performance Assessment Process. Your role in tracking teacher change extends to supervision and the summative evaluation involved in annual performance assessment. This process starts with teachers individually setting initial annual goals for their performance and professional development, which include at least one anti-bias goal. Goals should build on the individual teacher's existing skills and knowledge. It is best if the teachers take the initiative in the supervision process by identifying their goals and articulating a plan to meet them. However, there are times when you should step in to identify specific areas of concern a teacher has not recognized.

As teachers meet their initial annual goals, they should work with you to revise and identify new goals. This assessment process draws on the ongoing supervision you provide for each teacher, which should include a plan for regular observation in the classroom and ongoing dialogue (see Chapter 6 for more details). As with any area of teacher performance, you can hold teachers accountable to meet a basic level of competency in anti-bias skills and knowledge. This requires that you articulate these skills and dispositions as observable behaviors and that the teachers are aware of these expectations in advance.

DOCUMENTING CHILDREN'S LEARNING AND DEVELOPMENT

Classroom teachers have the primary responsibility for documenting and reflecting on children's growth in meeting anti-bias education goals. They are the ones who use these data to make decisions about their work with each child. Your responsibility includes setting expectations for documenting and planning for children's anti-bias learning, suggesting documentation strategies, providing professional development, and supervising teachers' work. You should expect teachers to include anti-bias goals in their progress reports and conferences with families.

Indicators of Children's Change

While the documentation and assessment of children's development is not the focus of this book, we do suggest guidelines for ongoing assessment of children. Ultimately, a program's impact on children's development and learning is one important window into the leader's efficacy. The anti-bias education goals for children fall under several learning and development domains, including social studies, social–emotional development, and cognitive development. If your state early learning standards include relevant and specific anti-bias criteria, you can incorporate these into your documentation and reporting process (see further discussion about this strategy in Chapter 9).

The following broad indicators of children's change are organized according to the four anti-bias education goals (Derman-Sparks & Edwards, 2010). It may be necessary to adjust the indicators we suggest to make them developmentally appropriate to the age group and cultural backgrounds of the children.

Goal 1. Each child will demonstrate self-awareness, confidence, family pride, and positive social identities.

- Identifies own physical characteristics (e.g., skin color, eye color, hair color and type)
- Uses home language at school
- Talks about home life at school

Goal 2. Each child will express comfort and joy with human diversity; accurate language for human differences; and deep, caring human connections.

- Notices similarities and differences in peers. For instance, a child comments, "We all talk but in different ways."
- Uses accurate language to describe differences. For instance, a child comments, "Isolena has two mommies."
- Recognizes strengths and challenges of each person. For instance, a child comments, "We all have things we are good at, and we all have things that are hard to do" or "Jinan has cerebral palsy; he can read, but it is hard for him to play tag."

Goal 3. Each child will increasingly recognize unfairness, have language to describe unfairness, and understand that unfairness hurts.

- Recognizes exclusion of another child. For instance, on the playground a child notices when a child is left out of a game, or inside when a child wants to join learning-center play.
- Recognizes stereotypes about people or behaviors related to her life that are depicted in objects in her environment. For instance, a child notices that a book doesn't show her family's constellation or that a greeting card has a stereotypical "Indian" in feathers and colored red.

Goal 4. Each child will demonstrate empowerment and the skills to act, with others or alone, against prejudice and/or discriminatory actions.

- Stands up for himself and others when he notices something is unfair. For instance, a child comments, "We cannot leave out Abraham just because he cannot run as fast as the other kids. His leg braces slow him down a little."
- Recognizes fair and unfair behaviors in the program environment. For instance, children notice that welcome signs and labeling of the learning material shelves are only in English. Kindergartners read about activism in history, such as during the civil rights movement, and then look at activism in their own lives and community.

- Contributes to finding a solution to an unfair situation. For instance, a small group of children find a way to change their game of Hokey Pokey so that a friend using a wheelchair can participate.

Another useful resource is a list of ECCE learning objectives developed by Stacey York in her book *Roots and Wings* (2003; see pp. 138–142). Teaching Tolerance (2013), a project of the Southern Poverty Law Center, has also developed a "Teaching Tolerance Anti-Bias Framework" for children in Grades K–2. Its standards and outcomes for identity, diversity, justice, and action are useful for kindergarten and primary-age children, but not directly applicable to preschool children.

Strategies for Observing Anti-Bias Growth

Teachers (and program leaders) use observation protocols and checklists, as well as ongoing curriculum documentation strategies (such as audio-recording children's conversations and photography) to reflect on what children are learning. The following specific strategies are useful for observing anti-bias indicators:

- Identify and record group discussions (comments, questions) that are likely to include reference to anti-bias concepts and behaviors. This includes learning experiences teachers have developed to provoke children's thinking and questions about the various aspects of differences and similarities among themselves, discussion about children's books and persona doll stories, responses to guest speakers, and problem solving around conflicts between children that include negative comments about identity.
- Identify times in the day and areas in the classroom that often involve examples of children's inclusion and exclusion of other children. What language, nonverbal behaviors, and gestures do children use? Who is being excluded or included in the play?
- Identify and observe for key words that children use in their attempts to understand difference, bias, and equity.
- Pay attention to gaps in children's understanding of diversity, especially the concepts they create that reflect misunderstanding or lack of information and their use of stereotypes of any aspects of diversity.

DOCUMENTING AND ASSESSING THE PROGRAM CULTURE

The program leader keeps a finger on the pulse of the overall program (Greenman, 1995) in relation to anti-bias change. This includes program policy, budgeting, family participation, support networks, and program visibility. Experienced leaders develop a gut-level sense of what is happening by being aware and observant of indicators of change. Even so, your intuition is *not* a substitute for systematic documentation, although it sometimes alerts you to specific issues that need your attention. Given all the demands on the program leader, it is a challenge to be systematic in documenting shifts in the overall culture of your program, so you need to create a way to do this that works for you. The initial reading of the program at the beginning of the school year provides a baseline for assessing overall changes (see Chapter 3).

Indicators of Program Change

We have separated the indicators into three broad areas: (1) Evidence of welcoming and including all members of the community, (2) changes in the structural elements of the program, such as policies, budgeting, and approach to regulations, and (3) the visibility of the program's anti-bias approach.

Creating Community: Welcoming and Including Everyone

- Visuals welcome and include all families, such as signs in different languages, images of diverse families, and posters declaring the program's support of equity and inclusion.
- The staff increasingly reflects the diversity of the families and surrounding neighborhood. For John's program in rural New Hampshire, this indicator was an ongoing challenge. While understanding that the role of context in a lack of progress was significant, John did not accept this as an "excuse" and continued to look at creative ways to keep working on this aspect of change.
- Families use their home languages with children, staff, and other families when at the program. They request and get translation assistance when needed.
- There is a shift to greater diversity in the demographics of the families. John and Debbie tracked changes in the social demographics of the families over many years.
- Families that do not represent the cultural mainstream are visible at program events and participate in a range of leadership opportunities. In contrast, some staff and families from dominant cultural groups may claim that they now feel left out. Even though they are still fully included, they may feel discomfort because they are no longer the only group that is visible and active in the program's community. The leader's role is to help families and staff understand their responses to shifts in the culture of the program.

Structural Elements of the Program Support Diversity

- There is evidence of an anti-bias filter (considering anti-bias values and goals) in decision making about all aspects of the program.
- Policies are not set in stone ("this is the way we do things") but are open to revision or modification in response to the diverse needs of the community.
- The program budget includes both regular and targeted resources for anti-bias efforts, including resources for special-needs inclusion, diversification of children's books and materials, translation services, and other resources for families.
- There is evidence of finding creative alternatives to deal with challenges to diversity created by external regulations and standards. For instance, the teachers work with families to create a more welcoming routine for washing children's hands on arrival that allows for cultural differences and still meets the accreditation criterion.

Visibility of Anti-Bias Values and Mission

- The program has an increasingly diverse network of relationships with community organizations that support its anti-bias work.
- The program has recognition in the broader community for its work on and advocacy of anti-bias education. This could be through stories in the local press, sharing curriculum documentation through the program website or a public venue, or by participating in activism in the neighborhood. On the flip side, this kind of visibility brings with it the possibility of misunderstanding or political opposition.

Tools for Documenting Change in the Program Culture

Many of the strategies and activities detailed in Chapters 4, 5, and 6 provide a program leader (and other stakeholders) with opportunities to pay attention to indicators of change. These activities and media include the use of storyboards, bulletin board displays, exhibitions, electronic media (blogs, websites), newsletters, and other documentation of classroom curriculum and staff professional development on anti-bias education. Other tools and processes that are useful in documenting change in the program culture are detailed below.

Revisiting Programwide Goals. Staff (and families) can develop and reach consensus on programwide anti-bias goals at the beginning of each year. For instance, an anti-bias goal could be: *Develop a clearer understanding of the resources* *and capacity needed to ensure that the program is inclusive of all abilities.* The staff then revisits the program goals, preferably at midyear and prior to the development of new annual goals. The purpose is to discuss, and document in writing, evidence of concrete actions the staff has taken in meeting these goals. John offers this description of his procedure for goal review:

I asked individual staff members and classroom teams to submit specific examples of progress. At the spring retreat, I also formed cross-team small groups to discuss and share actions they and the center as a whole had taken to meet a specific goal. I pooled and organized all the feedback, and distributed it to the staff and the parent advisory committee so they could reflect on what they had accomplished together. I found that the dialogue that unfolded during this reflection process was as valuable as the final documentation.

Annual Family Survey. Questions specific to your anti-bias efforts should be included in the annual family survey and the findings shared and discussed with the various stakeholders. Depending on the content and group, the leader might decide to share the raw data (with personal or inappropriate material removed) or create a more manageable summary. At John's program, he was strategic in beginning with intentionally broad questions that parents could interpret in many ways: *Our center is seeking to be more effective in providing a program that respects diversity and promotes equity in all that it does. How effective are we? What feedback do you have regarding this goal?*

I felt that this broad wording would give me both a "read" on the families' understanding of diversity and equity in an ECCE program and a sense of the range of views about this work. Over the years, there had also been specific ideas and feedback that alerted us to both changes we needed to make and varying perceptions of our work. For instance, parents had asked us to work on gender inclusion on the playground, the need for greater diversity among our teachers, and being more proactive about informing parents about events in the community. On the flip side, I had also read comments that indicated some parents saw "diversity" as focusing on countries and cultures around the world, a few who viewed it as "biased," and others who simply had not thought about the issue. When a parent wrote "The question is so broad I have no idea how to reply!" I realized it was time to be more explicit about our use of the term "anti-bias" and include specific questions focused on current initiatives.

Debbie took a different approach at EPCS:

I chose to have a separate anti-bias education section in the survey because of the school's long history with this work. Questions included:

- What have you learned as a member of an anti-bias education community?
- What have your children learned as members of an anti-bias education community?

- What has been challenging for your family?
- What have been the benefits for your family?

Community Dialogue Prompts. In contrast to the individuality and anonymity of surveys, the program leader can invent more interactive strategies to collect feedback from community members. For instance, Debbie reports the following:

At the end of the program year, we used the entranceway bulletin board to post this prompt, "What have I learned about being a member of an anti-bias community?" The display included responses the teachers had written on cardboard circles during an earlier staff meeting. Materials were provided so family members (and other visitors) could also add comments.

This kind of public documentation not only provides a source of community feedback but also shows the program's accountability to its anti-bias education mission.

Anti-Bias Education Forum and Exhibit. The following event from Debbie's program, also discussed in Chapter 6, offers a window into an in-depth process of sharing anti-bias efforts and collecting feedback from all stakeholders. Rather than an annual event, we see this as an example of what an experienced program can do at longer intervals as a way of focusing its efforts and taking stock of its cutting edge in this work. Debbie explains:

The process centered on a 2-year programwide inquiry into anti-bias education that included classroom curriculum and a parallel process of teacher professional development. Families were also engaged in the inquiry through their individual classrooms and programwide groups. During the 2nd year, there were several vehicles for dissemination of the work and inviting feedback, including a program newsletter, a community forum, and a concluding exhibit and gallery walk.

The program held the exhibit and gallery walk over the course of 2 weeks and included the following:

- An *opening celebration* at which the program leader gave a talk and invited outside guests to provide commentary on the exhibit.
- *Documentation panels* on each classroom's curriculum, focused on a different area of social identity.
- *Identity Webs:* A wall of identity webs by staff and teachers, with an invitation to participants to add their own web and respond to the prompt, *How does my identity influence my role as an educator, parent, or caregiver?*
- *Chalk Talk:* An interactive graffiti wall on which participants could share their responses to the following prompt: *In what ways does anti-bias work build or challenge a school community?*

Community Network Mapping. Program leaders can map and assess their network of community supporters (individuals and organizations) on an annual basis using the following questions:

- What ABE resources does each organization/individual offer?
- How have we used these resources as part of anti-bias education efforts in the past year?
- In what ways have we been able to provide support to the organizations/individuals?
- What other community organizations/individuals could we access through this network to support ABE efforts?

A NECESSARY ELEMENT IN CREATING CHANGE

Careful documentation of your progress in creating an anti-bias community is critical to creating future strategies and plans. On a more personal level, we see this process as an important opportunity to celebrate your own and the community's efforts and successes along the way. Change is a long-term undertaking and program leaders do not always see the fruits of their commitment to an anti-bias vision. A clear picture of where you have been and where you are now in the journey helps sustain you through future challenges.

In Chapter 9 we widen our lens to examine a new challenge: the increasing use of required standards and assessments in the early childhood field. In particular we focus on their relevance to and impact on the work of growing an anti-bias approach at your program.

Anti-Bias Education in a Climate of Required Standards and Assessments

We must think of standards as the floor for our work, not the ceiling
—Catherine Goins (personal communication, 2014)

Every state in the nation now has early learning guidelines or standards describing learning outcomes for children below kindergarten age; a majority has or is in the process of developing linked assessment tools (Scott-Little, Lesko, Martello, & Milburn, 2007). The Office of Head Start (2010) has instituted the Child Development and Early Learning Framework, and children in the early years of public schooling (K–3) are accountable to district and state learning outcomes, often including the Common Core State Standards (CCSS; National Governors Association Center for Best Practices & Council of Chief State School Officers, 2010). In their 2002 joint position statement, the National Association for the Education of Young Children (NAEYC) and the National Association of Early Childhood Specialists in State Departments of Education (NAECS/SDE) concluded that "early childhood education has become part of a standards-based environment. . . .This movement presents both opportunities and challenges for early childhood education" (p. 1).

Programs in many states *also* navigate through program standards, Quality Rating Improvement Systems (QRIS), which are often tied to funding, and government mandates for assessing program quality at the state and federal levels. In addition, programs may seek to assess and improve their practices by going through an accreditation process offered by a national organization such as NAEYC. Unlike standards and assessments that focus on children's learning in order to guide teaching and curriculum choices, these program standards are intended for monitoring a program's effectiveness in providing quality education as part of accountability to families, administration, and policymakers.

In sum, a plethora of externally developed learning and program standards documents and assessment tools exist. They vary considerably in regards to their incorporation of child development research, the ECCE field's best practices, and attention to diversity issues. While some of the published standards and assessment tools include criteria on diversity, and a handful contain criteria specifically addressing anti-bias issues, many ignore diversity and anti-bias education and development as components of quality early childhood education. To complicate matters further, learning and program standards and assessment tools are also in a state of flux, as early childhood educators, researchers, and politicians provide feedback and demand changes.

The benefit or threat (or perhaps both) of required standards and assessments in the improvement of early childhood education is a hotly contested topic, with educators, families, researchers, community activists, and politicians on different sides of the issues. A major concern of many early childhood educators is the lack of developmental appropriateness in many learning standards and assessment tools. In addition, many critics also express apprehension that the overemphasis on testing and assessment can come at the expense of other aspects of early childhood education (Carlsson-Paige, 2010). They further worry that teachers are becoming increasingly dependent on scripted curriculum that focuses on children doing well on tests, rather than on developing their skills of child observation and providing curriculum tailored to individual needs. A related concern is that an over-focus on learning standards and standardized assessments "are promoting a de-professionalization of teachers. Their ability to provide the optimal, individualized learning opportunities they know how to offer make way for prescribed curricula taught in lock step to all children" (Carlsson-Paige, 2010, p. 1).

Even when educators criticize learning standards and the associated assessments, most also make clear that having benchmarks for children's development and ways to assess their growth is not in itself the problem. These can help teachers ensure that their practice with each child does indeed further learning. They argue that assessments "should help teachers focus on children's natural developmental progression and variations, and should be used to help teachers better support children's learning" (Weingarten & Carlsson-Paige, 2013, p. 1).

Given this environment, a number of early childhood teachers and program leaders are questioning if they can still also implement anti-bias education. We believe that it *is* possible. The aim of this chapter is to offer strategies and support for continuing to build quality anti-bias programs in the face of required standards and assessments for children and programs. We conclude by offering information about ways to join in the ongoing discussion and activism about standards and assessments. Throughout, we draw on insights from experienced early childhood educators and leaders, especially the following:

- Catherine Goins, Associate Superintendent of Early Education and Administration, Placer County Office of Education, California
- Luis Hernandez, Early Childhood Education Specialist, Training and Technical Assistance Services, Head Start, Western Kentucky University
- Peter Mangione, Codirector, Center for Child and Family Studies, WestEd, California
- Mary Pat Martin, Professor of Early Childhood Education, Oakton Community College, Illinois

Louise interviewed these educators during April and May, 2013. Their experiences of overseeing state and federal ECCE programs, including Head Start, as well as engaging in training teachers, provide them with practical strategies grounded in real experiences and knowledge about ways people around the country manage standards and assessments. We hope their ideas will help you be creatively strategic in doing anti-bias education in the context of your program's particular required standards and assessments, whatever they may be. We also hope that you will realize that you are not alone in doing this work.

WORKING STRATEGICALLY IN YOUR ECCE PROGRAM

While program leaders have to deal with external standards and assessments, they do not have to succumb to them. As Luis Hernandez aptly put it, they must find solutions, in their particular settings, to "Take a lemon and turn it into lemonade. Leadership and being strategic is key, key, key, key, key."

Productively and creatively working with any of the forms of required or even voluntary standards and assessment systems is more likely to happen when staff has a strong foundation in child development, early learning, and individualized teaching. Program leaders and staff also need the values we discuss in previous chapters, such as believing that every child and family must be visible, feel that they belong, and have a role to play in the program. In addition, the program leader and staff must engage in internal work about their assumptions, biases, and points of view.

Here is a range of practical strategies for "making lemonade out of lemons" that is drawn from interviews about standards and assessments with the early childhood leaders identified above.

Do Your Homework

Inform yourself about appropriate assessment for young children in general and about possible negative consequences of inappropriate assessment. One place to begin is by studying *Early Childhood Assessment: Why, What, and How,* the National Research Council's 2008 report on child assessment that emphasizes both the positive aspects of assessment as well as cautions about misuse. NAEYC's position statement on *Early Childhood Curriculum, Assessment, and Program Evaluation* (developed in collaboration with NAECS/SDE), and their *Basics of Assessment: A Primer for Early Childhood Professionals* (McAfee, Leong, & Bodrova, 2004) offer definitions and analyses of the various kinds of program and learning standards and assessments. Feeney and Freeman (2014) suggest ways to tackle the issue of kindergarten standardized testing in their *Young Children* article, "Focus on Ethics."

Just as you "read" all other components of the program (as we discuss in Chapter 3), you also look critically at the specifics of the program and learning standards and assessment tools that your program uses. Identify whether the criteria, content, and expectations in standards are developmentally and cultur-ally appropriate and the assessment strategies are ethical and appropriate for all children (NAEYC/NAECS/SDE, 2002). In addition, consider if the standards and assessment tools you use include strong supports for early childhood pro-grams, professionals, and families, and multiple ways to assess the children.

From an anti-bias perspective, most existing assessment tools do not ad-equately evaluate programs on their diversity and equity work, if at all. Look for any criteria that directly, or even indirectly, address diversity issues. The language for these criteria may vary; what matters is that they do address diversity issues. If the criteria in your program's assessment tool disregard diversity and anti-bias goals, then having your own documentation data be-comes particularly important to make the case for the program's effectiveness and congruence with best practices (see Chapter 8).

Be Well Grounded in the ECCE Knowledge Base

Knowing current research about child development, including the cri-tiques from the perspective of cultural diversity, is an essential element in an anti-bias educator's repertoire. So too is being well versed in the construc-tion of social identity and prejudice. If the required standards your program works with reflect awareness of this knowledge base, then you can use them to support aspects of anti-bias work. In several states, early childhood educators were members of the committees that created standards and were able to in-clude criteria the field accepts as best practices. Peter Mangione, who directed California's development of ECCE's state foundations, explained:

We had enough research to understand that children belong to and participate in numerous groups, and to the different kinds of experiences they have with others. This allowed us to not just focus on the individual self when we looked at founda-tions for self-awareness and self-concept.

Some program standards call for practices such as individualization and family engagement, while some learning standards include positive self-concept development and learning cooperative social interaction skills. Luis Hernandez, who has worked with and trained Head Start staff throughout the Southeast for many years, argues that standards with a focus on the individualization of learn-ing and development open the door to looking at children in the context of their family, home life, community, gender, and class. From this perspective, there is room to address diversity by individualizing teaching and learning. In addition, standards for social–emotional development and for social science curriculum, which several states also include, have elements conducive to diversity.

Treat the Standards as the Floor, Not the Ceiling!

Catherine Goins finds that the program-leader attitude that poses the most threat to anti-bias work—indeed, to quality education in general—is treating standards as setting the limit of what a program does. She explains what that means to her as director of early childhood programs in one of the larger counties in California:

I am hearing that attention will only be given to what is required—not to what is not. My position is that, standards only are the minimum requirements of what we have to do. No rating scale can capture everything, nor does simply teaching to the assessment tool carry out our professional responsibilities to children and families. If we treat them as a limit or our only goals, then once we get to them, it is unlikely that we will have culturally responsive and anti-bias education. Nothing stops you from doing anti-bias education if you know it well.

As with standards, the key to dealing with externally mandated assessment tools (measuring both child and program) is to treat them as the floor, not the ceiling of your work. Avoid the trap of treating these assessments as the ceiling and only teaching to their criteria. Nothing stops you from continuing to implement the best knowledge and practices of the ECCE field in your program, which includes anti-bias education.

Build Upon Any Criteria and Language about Diversity and Inclusiveness

Some state learning and program standards, as well as national Head Start requirements, include specific items about diversity issues, such as family culture, home language, and inclusiveness. Although these indicators are usually insufficient, anti-bias educators, as Luis Hernandez advises, must learn how to use the language that *is* there to make a bridge to anti-bias goals and aspirations. Peter Mangione agrees, stating, "Even though the California Foundations does not include details about doing diversity and equity work, its general framework does invite teachers to think about how to support identity and attitude formation of children."

Finally, as mentioned earlier, Catherine Goins asserts,

While I want the anti-bias principles to be embedded throughout the standards documents, if you have grounding in anti-bias education, nothing keeps you from exceeding the suggestions about diversity and inclusiveness. As long as people can articulate what they are doing, even if they do not use the examples, they can score high.

Identify Connections between Standards Criteria and Anti-Bias Goals

This strategy relies on a strong grounding in best ECCE practices and in anti-bias education. It requires the program leader to carefully search through the standards with an anti-bias lens, identifying where specific criteria intersect with anti-bias goals and curriculum. In states where early childhood educators served on the committees that developed their state's standards, at least some criteria reflect what the field is thinking about child development and best practices. Use standards such as individualization, family engagement, positive self-concept development, and learning cooperative social-interaction skills for anti-bias work. The items related to social science curriculum are another place to find diversity and equity issues.

It also is crucial to involve staff in finding, analyzing, and navigating these connections (see the examples at the end of the chapter). Then staff can build on these in a meaningful way, thereby continuing to do anti-bias education, while also addressing standards.

Do Your Own Program Assessment

The previous chapter describes methods for gathering several kinds of information throughout the school year that enables the program leader to assess the state of anti-bias work at any given point in time and where it needs to go next. Whether or not a program has required assessment tools, it is important to implement an ongoing assessment plan congruent with the principles of diversity and anti-bias education. The purpose for doing so is twofold:

1. Appropriate assessment makes it possible to keep improving the quality of the program's work.
2. Having meaningful information about the program's anti-bias work provides a way for the leader to advocate for the program's mission.

Use Standardized Assessment Tools That Support Anti-Bias Work

One of the most widely used tools for program assessment that does include diversity items is the *Early Childhood Environment Rating Scale*, revised edition (Harms, Clifford, & Cryer, 2005). To get an acceptable or good score on the ECERS-R, there must be some evidence of either racial or cultural diversity that is obvious to children. To get the highest score, programs have to show inclusion and diversity as part of children's play and daily activities. However, our interviewees suggest that it is still necessary to look carefully at the examples for diversity activities, since some of them reflect a "tourist multicultural" approach (Derman-Sparks & Edwards, 2010).

A new supplement to the ECERS-R, the ECERS-E (Sylva, Siraj-Blatchford, & Taggart, 2011), offers a much improved breakdown of the criteria for a range of ratings on diversity work.

It includes the first anti-bias language in nationally used assessment tools. Coauthored by Iram Siraj-Blatchford, an early childhood antiracism educator in the United Kingdom, the ECERS-E identifies very specific behaviors for a diversity component, which correspond to anti-bias education goals. This component assesses how much staff takes into account the needs of "children of different genders, cultural/ethnic groups, and varying levels of ability," using three measures: Planning for Individual Learning Needs, Gender Equality and Awareness, and Race Equality and Awareness (Sylva et al., 2011, p. 5):

1. *Planning for Individual Learning Needs* (Items 44–45) looks for program evidence that support children of all developmental stages and backgrounds to participate in all aspects of the program, including individual and group activities. This component also scores whether planned activities encourage children to explore differences and abilities in a positive way (e.g., exploring various disabilities and adaptation in themes about the body).
2. *Gender Equality and Awareness* (Items 46–47) looks for evidence that the learning materials enable children to learn about the range of nonstereotypical roles for men and women and that activities help children discuss the range of gender roles and participate in non-gender-stereotypical activities. To achieve a high score, there also must be evidence that the staff challenges and guides children in discussion of stereotypical behaviors and assumptions.
3. *Race Equality and Awareness* (Items 48–49) requires that programs have culturally diverse staff and intentionally promote children exploring similarities and differences in things, people, and their families' cultures. A high score requires that exploration of similarities and differences are routinely woven into learning projects or unit themes, and that staff know how to intervene when children or adults behave in a prejudicial or discriminatory manner.

Whether or not the ECERS-R is the mandated assessment tool for your program, the ECERS-E is a useful tool for anti-bias work. Draw on it to improve staff's work with the children and for communicating with external evaluators about how your anti-bias activities relate to program standards.

Be Able to Explain Your Anti-Bias Work to Outside Evaluators or Regulators

Do your homework so that you can show how anti-bias education curriculum activities relate to specific standards (e.g., "Here is how we work on children developing a strong sense of self or learning to interact respectfully"). Material in NAEYC's *Developmentally appropriate practice in early childhood programs* (Copple & Bredekamp, 2009), and its *Responding to linguistic and cultural diversity: Recommendations for effective early childhood education* position statement (NAEYC, 1995), provide support for anti-bias education as part of best practices. In addition, know how to explain your internal documentation and assessment process regarding your anti-bias work (see Chapter 8). The goal is to convince colleagues, administrators, and families that an anti-bias education approach makes it possible to implement more fully the required standards.

Say No to Feeling Overwhelmed or Powerless

Program leaders' attitudes are central to effectively managing required program and learning standards and assessments. The leader does not have to do it alone, but rather works together with staff to meet these demands without undermining the program's ideas about quality, including its anti-bias mission and goals. "It is important for teachers [and the program leader] to have confidence that an intentionally designed hands-on curriculum can address standards effectively while preparing children with the knowledge and skills they are expected to acquire. That means that ethical teachers will resist the temptation to teach to the test and will avoid overemphasizing test-taking skills to the exclusion of other worthwhile content" (Feeney & Freeman, 2014, p. 87).

Educating families about the challenges that standards and assessment tools pose for your program and how staff are meeting these, without sacrificing the program's mission, is part of not feeling powerless. The kind of standards a program must use does affect the leader's flexibility. It is much harder to adapt standards that rest on an either/or framework than those that offer guidelines while allowing for individualization. However, it is important to remember that standards do not typically address implementation, leaving decisions about how to implement each standard to programs. This allows for creativity as the program leader and teachers use their knowledge about how children develop identity and learn about cultural diversity. Program leaders can avoid the trap of thinking that standards mean ensuring that everything is systemized and the same, and instead, encourage teachers to adapt what they do to the needs of real children and families.

ACTIVISM BEYOND YOUR PROGRAM

Whether standards and related assessment play a meaningful role in defining and improving the quality of early childhood programs is still unclear. Whether it is possible for one-size-fits-all standards and assessment tools to incorporate the diverse cultural contexts of development and multiple ways young children develop and learn is a critical question for the field of early childhood education. It is also critical for our nation. The increasing role of corporate business in producing and selling for-profit, one-size-fits-all curriculum and assessment materials is worrisome (Karp, 2013–2014). These materials promise high assessment scores while often ignoring what the ECCE field views as best practice based on research about development.

In the short term, program leaders and staff must deal with standards and assessment tools as well as they can. To change the landscape of standards and assessments beyond one's own program, it is vital to work collaboratively with other early childhood professionals, families, and interested people in general. Figuring out ways to be strategic about managing these standards and assessments is much more effective when working with others. Doing this with your staff is important, but not a substitute for networking with other program leaders. They bring a different perspective and can buoy you when you feel frustrated or powerless. Find like-minded colleagues through your local director's network and state professional conferences, or through setting up an online network for program leaders across your state.

Work with Your Local College ECCE Faculty

Connecting anti-bias education goals with standards in teacher training can build a pool of new teachers who have grounding in implementing anti-bias education in the climate of required standards. In her classes Mary Pat Martin, an anti-bias leader in Chicago and a community college faculty member, infuses anti-bias goals and issues into the Illinois Early Learning and Development Standards (Illinois State Board of Education, Division of Early Childhood, 2013).

She focuses on the Social Studies and the Social–Emotional Development standards. For example, the social studies standard for citizenship (#14A)— "understand what it means to be a member of a group and community"—includes several specific learning goals, one of which is "contribute to the well-being of one's early childhood environment, school, and community." These learning goals connect with all four ABE core goals. Specific issues to explore with children reflecting the anti-bias education goals are individual and social identity, relationships with people different from oneself, fairness and unfairness, and taking action to change unfairness.

Anti-bias goals also can easily connect with another social studies learning standard (#18A) that focuses on knowing about the similarities and differences in people. This includes being able to describe characteristics such as hair length, skin color, age, height, and so on of oneself and others. Anti-bias education additions include the ideas that we are all both alike and different and those differences are to be valued. Children's misinformation or discomforts about specific aspects of human characteristics may emerge, and become the starting place for further anti-bias curriculum.

The Illinois Social–Emotional Development standards also offer several connecting points with anti-bias goals. Consider the standard (#31A) about having the social awareness and interpersonal skills to establish and maintain positive relationships, including showing empathy, sympathy, and caring for others. If program leaders have done their homework about anti-bias education, then they can easily see the intersections with their required standards.

To analyze the potential intersecting points between anti-bias education and standards, Mary Pat Martin first engages her college students in thoroughly exploring the meaning and activity possibilities of the four core anti-bias goals. Second, they examine the Illinois Standards for direct and indirect reflections of the four anti-bias goals. They find indicators for goals one and two, but nothing for goals three and four, which involve critical thinking and activism. Third, they examine their community college handout of ECE Curricular Goals and Objectives. As a result of Mary Pat Martin's work with her early childhood department colleagues, these goals and objectives incorporate anti-bias language. This process of analysis becomes the foundation for students' development of lesson plans that integrate anti-bias goals with required standards.

Join with Colleagues in Your Community and Beyond

As an anti-bias leader, you will need to become familiar and comfortable with advocating for change beyond your program.

To start, participate in the discussions and advocacy efforts of professional organizations such as the Association for Childhood International and NAEYC, and national advocacy organizations such as the Alliance for Childhood (www.allianceforchildren.org) and Defending the Early Years (DEY) (www.deyproject.org). You can stay up-to-date on current developments with information and materials from these advocacy groups. DEY offers an Early Childhood Activist Toolkit, with informational and action resources, created with the help of early childhood educators around the country. Ideas for actions include organizing a Call Your Legislator Day, spearheading a letter-writing campaign to politicians, and organizing a "play-in" at the local school board meeting. The objectives of Defending the Early Years (DEY, n.d.) are the following:

1. To mobilize the early childhood community to speak out with well-reasoned arguments against inappropriate standards, assessments, and classroom practices
2. To track the effects of new standards, especially those linked to the Common Core State Standards, on early childhood education policy and practice (This objective is specifically relevant to K–3 educators)
3. To promote appropriate practices in early childhood classrooms and support educators in counteracting current reforms which undermine these appropriate practices

Get involved in public efforts to protect young children from the potential ill effects of inappropriate assessments. Work with colleagues through the local affiliate of your professional organization (e.g., AEYC) to carry out these activities. The following strategies are additional ways you can be actively involved in the debate regarding required standards and assessments (Feeney & Freeman, 2014):

• Write letters to your local newspapers about the issues involved in developing and implementing appropriate program and learning standards and assessment practices.

- Present workshops or panels for families about issues in assessment.
- Provide written or oral testimony regarding relevant legislation at the state and federal levels.
- Work with state departments responsible for early learning standards (e.g., Education or Health and Human Services), by serving on task forces and giving feedback on draft standards during the public comment period.

John describes his experience working with the taskforce in New Hampshire:

This work gave me the opportunity to influence the development of the standards with anti-bias values in mind and to develop a network of allies. In particular, I advocated successfully for the inclusion of clear language regarding dual-language learners and made sure those examples and expectations were appreciative of differences in culture and ability. Along with colleagues on the taskforces, I worked to ensure that appropriate language regarding children's social identity development was included. While there is still a long way to go toward truly reflecting all the anti-bias goals in the standards, we made a start and engaged in an important dialogue with stakeholders from across the state.

TAKING ON THE ISSUES

Having to juggle required learning and program standards and assessments with anti-bias education is demanding. It adds more complexity and tasks to program leaders' already very full plates. The push for one-size-fits-all standards and assessment tools seems to formalize and heighten existing contested issues. It also opens doors to the "corporatization" of early childhood curriculum. Perhaps that is the new threat to equitable care and education for all children (Karp, 2013–2014).

Building a program based on children's developmental stages, individual rhythms, active learning, the essential connection between the cognitive and emotional modalities, and attention to the role of culture in growth and learning, requires constant diligence. So too does attention to challenging the limits that prejudice and discrimination of all kinds can place on children developing their full potential. Commitment to this work includes finding ways to use, change, or contain required program and learning standards and assessments so they do not undermine what is best for all children. Achieving success requires collaborating with colleagues, families, other professionals, and community people. Our experience tells us that while this takes our time, it also is critical to sustaining ourselves over the long haul of building anti-bias early childhood programs.

CHAPTER 10

Sustaining the Anti-Bias Vision

Reflections

How do people who lead anti-bias education programs keep up their energy and commitment over time? What sustains them? In this final chapter, we share several themes from Debbie's and John's reflections on their many years of experience directing in a variety of early childhood settings. We end with Louise's reflections on her long-time work as a national and international anti-bias education author, educator, and consultant.

"MAN MAN LAI": SLOWLY IT WILL COME

This traditional Chinese maxim means "Appreciate the small steps that lead to bigger movement." It is probably the most important of all the principles underpinning anti-bias work and leadership. As Debbie and John point out, practicing it is not easy:

John: I feel uneasy that we are not doing enough to move anti-bias work forward. I have to remind myself that anti-bias change is incremental and long range.

Debbie: It helps to pay attention to the "small changes" and to keep reminding ourselves that our work is a step-by-step process. When the work gets really complicated or frustrating, I break down the problem, just focus on one aspect for today, and not worry about all the other pieces until another day. In other words, it is useful to take one day at a time—sometimes even one hour at a time.

John: In the end, what matters most is balancing a sense of urgency and impatience: the call to act, with the patience to be in it for the long haul.

MOTIVATION COMES FROM OUR INNER CORE

We all agree that doing anti-bias work is inseparable from who we are. Debbie explains:

I always felt on the outside, growing up third-generation Chinese American in predominantly White communities. My firsthand experiences of feeling different, being ostracized and the target of bias and racism, resulted in my becoming an activist. There was a period when I felt like I did not belong anywhere. These feelings motivated me to create communities that celebrate differences and are safe and inclusive places for all children and families. At the same time, I also wanted to build a community that was "safe" for my own growing multiracial family.

John adds his perspective:

For me, taking on anti-bias leadership is a natural extension of my core values of respect for others and a love of diversity in the human experience. It is a part of who I am. It is hard for me to imagine *not* doing this work. This work opens me up to the experiences of people who have so much to offer me in terms of perspectives and experiences. To me, diversity of experience and the willingness to step outside of your comfort zone are essential to learning and growth.

As a White, upper-middle-class male, I believe that I am particularly aware of the importance of anti-bias goals to children who are growing up with access to power in this society. I also believe that my racial, gender, and social class privilege requires me to look carefully at my assumptions and biases. I know, for example, that my upper-middle-class background has sometimes meant that I don't truly appreciate or understand the way a lack of resources may affect families and staff members. Over the years, I have found it helpful to ask myself, "Where am I coming from, and where is the other person coming from? How can I understand and respond to the emotions and perspectives of people who have a different history and identity to me?"

WE DRAW ON DREAMS AND ON STRATEGY

Our dreams and hopes give us motivation, direction, and persistence. At the same time, experience has taught us about the critical importance of strategy—and the reality of expecting small changes. Change requires creative visioning, risk taking, and strategic decision making based on thoughtful analysis. John relates:

I drew inspiration from the dreamers and visionaries around me. My challenge is that sometimes my desire to know how we will accomplish our mission limits my imagination and creativity. Anti-bias education requires both creativity and a willingness to dream big.

Initially a dream of two of the teachers, a beautiful mural created at CSDC is one example of doing this. All of the staff, children, and families worked with a local artist to paint a mural that represented the center's vision about diversity in a very public way. The teachers convinced the artist, Richard Haynes, a man with a very different cultural background from the children's, and who had never worked with preschoolers, to undertake a 3-month apprenticeship with the children. They also secured a grant from the Teaching Tolerance organization to support the initiative. Over the course of a semester's work on the mural, the teachers, parents, and children engaged in conversations about race, racism, and the values of respect. They proudly erected the final mural, 6ft x 6ft, at the entrance and invited both the university and surrounding town to view it. John was aware of the challenges the mural project might bring, but he was perceptive enough to see a goal worth pursuing:

As the center leader, I gave support, encouragement, and resources to the project. In collaboration with the teachers, I also made sure to broadcast the work to the wider community by holding an official opening, attracting media attention, and by creating visual documentation at the center and on our website. Morris Dees, a social justice activist and a founder of Teaching Tolerance, even visited to see our work. The mural image has become a kind of logo for the program!

A JUGGLING ACT

The teacher as juggler metaphor is a familiar one in the education profession. That is also the case for the leader's role. Building an anti-bias program brings its own particular balls to juggle, along with those already part of your act. One new ball is paying attention to your overall anti-bias education work throughout the program. At the same time, every one of the balls representing the many elements of an early childhood care and education program (e.g., relations with families, curriculum, collegiality, assessment, accreditation, and community outreach) should include some aspect of anti-bias education. A never-ending balancing act is a necessary part of making choices about where to focus. John explains:

Sometimes I try to give myself a bit of a break in my focus on anti-bias work, especially when I need to focus on other aspects of the program, be it the math curriculum or ensuring the center is safe. I still make sure we maintain the anti-bias trajectory throughout the program. So, I try to balance making progress in anti-bias work—figuring out next steps—and keeping all the various parts of the program going.

Debbie uses the phrase, "rotated neglect" to explain this concept:

I remind the teachers and myself that we cannot do everything all at once. We just need to be sure it is not the same thing we are neglecting each time. I include personal and family time as part of the equation too. Don't let personal time be the one that is always neglected.

TRIUMPH OVER PERSONAL CHALLENGES

Looking back on her career of 40 plus years as a social justice educator, Debbie shares that many of the strengths she developed to lead anti-bias work took time:

As I got older, I also became more experienced, and, hopefully, wiser. My biggest challenge was learning to embrace conflict and disequilibrium as possibilities for growth. At first, it was very hard when everyone did not agree. I wanted to be open to different viewpoints, yet also hold to the core anti-bias values. It was difficult when I felt like I let someone down, or some people were not pleased with how it went, or people felt misunderstood when we disagreed, or I felt misunderstood. I took disappointment that we could not reach consensus as a personal rejection.

There were times when I could not let it go and brought the work home, waking up in the middle of the night upset with these feelings. I got tired. Eventually, I stopped seeing everything as right or wrong, and accepted that most things are more complicated and nuanced than that. I learned to identify and accept people where they are and to feel good about helping them move along. I do believe in and have bottom lines, but I can also agree to disagree and let some things go. Over the years I have found more balance—no longer expecting a transformation to happen overnight, appreciating the small steps of change and movement. I was able to handle the long haul with optimism.

John reflects on other challenges:

As a leader, you are in a vulnerable position because it is part of your job to stand by the teachers, families, and anti-bias values. This public role has made me feel vulnerable, especially when someone's objections to anti-bias change become emotional and personal. Part of my challenge is not to let my fears about what *might* happen when I take on difficult issues hold me back. Over the years, I have often been surprised, delighted, and humbled by the willingness of families and teachers to embrace change and to share their stories of dealing with bias.

TOP-DOWN AND BUBBLE-UP CHANGE

Anti-bias change requires both leadership and grass-roots investment. Both Debbie and John value and work from the principle that anti-bias change is an ongoing, dynamic interaction between the program leader and the program's stakeholders. As John explains:

I focus my efforts on creating a grassroots commitment to anti-bias values. This is very different from simply using my authority to *require* change. When a teacher suggests a book that the staff should read together, or a group of parents undertakes the facilitation of a diversity dialogue or training, or a teacher challenges my commitment to equity, these acts of initiative fuel my commitment.

I worked hard to find the right balance between directing (Do it this way), challenging (How could you do it differently?), and affirmation (You took a great risk in your practice!). I also thought a great deal about the parents and staff members who are silent about anti-bias change. What are they thinking and feeling? How could we engage in a dialogue? I try to be aware of and reach out to community members who may seem to be on the sidelines of anti-bias changes. Maybe they are going through their own process of disequilibrium and change.

Debbie adds:

Sometimes this concept of grassroots investment means giving up some power and sharing it with your staff. When I first came to the EPCS, I found that the previous director had planned and led the monthly staff meetings. I began shifting this model by instituting a staff survey on what topics they were interested in learning about in the upcoming year. Eventually we moved to having each classroom team be responsible for leading a staff meeting. The biggest change was the investment of staff in the staff meetings; they now felt ownership for the success of the staff meetings.

FINDING SUCCESS IN THE SMALL CHANGES

As we said earlier in this chapter, and in many ways throughout the book, anti-bias endeavors happen in small steps that lead to bigger movement. Observing and celebrating small changes around us help move that work forward. In the book we identify several benchmarks for assessing growth in anti-bias goals. Here, Debbie and John describe indicators that especially can tell leaders that the shift toward an anti-bias culture is happening. At EPCS Debbie looked for teachers and families dropping by her office or stopping her in the hall to share anti-bias stories from the classroom, in their personal lives, at home, or with the children. Debbie continues: "I know things are working when people are asking anti-bias questions, questioning status quo policies and practices in the school." John agrees:

When I heard folks spontaneously holding anti-bias conversations among themselves and feeling comfortable to talk with me about difficult topics, or even saying they disagree on an anti-bias issue—I knew things were shifting. I also felt successful that I was moving forward when people in groups who are targets of prejudice and discrimination came to trust me—-a trust I work hard to earn. I was always looking to learn something new from the people with whom I was working.

STAYING OVER THE LONG HAUL

As Debbie acknowledged in her reflections about personal challenges, from time to time anti-bias leaders like you get tired. Being thoughtful and paying attention to where the individuals you lead are in their own anti-bias journeys takes discipline and energy. Every so often you need to recoup.

Reminding yourself why you decided to do anti-bias education helps. Revisiting your vision and hopes for a better world can keep you going over the long haul. Acknowledging the anti-bias steps that have been taken and the growth that has occurred is equally necessary. It is too easy to beat yourself up about what you did not do, or did not do well, or what you wished you had achieved.

It is important to take care of yourself, whatever that may mean to you. Take a break, go for a walk, go to the gym, read a book, go to the movies, call a friend. Most especially, having a group of supportive colleagues can keep you going. For Debbie and John this meant good professional friends at work and around the globe. Debbie remarks:

My long-time colleagues, like John, became close friends over the years. No matter where any of us were, I felt I could pick up the phone or drop an email any time I wanted, and they would be there for me. At conferences and professional meetings, my lunches and check-ins with trusted colleagues outside my program were as important as the conference sessions and meeting topics. They sustained and nurtured me.

John adds:

When I experienced feeling unsure or inadequate about a given situation, or exhausted after dealing with a tense conflict situation, I sought out my closest allies and mentors. They inevitably reminded me of all the things I had achieved, the importance of my core values, and that change can unsettle people.

WHEN LEADERSHIP CHANGES

Does anti-bias transformation survive a change in program leadership? Every leader, in any setting, faces this question at some point in her or his career. The leader does matter, because as we say throughout this book, *leadership* matters. In early childhood programs (or in any organization), a new leader can and often does change the mission and focus of a program's work. Will the anti-bias changes endure?

John reflects on the significance of a long-term view in anti-bias efforts:

It is important to be at peace with the notion that you may not be around to see the realization of some of the change you are hoping for in your work. I directed my efforts at CSDC toward enduring and deep change. That is why I valued shared leadership (in the broader sense of the word), grassroots change, and a focus on relationships rather than things. I also looked at ways to create and institutionalize change throughout the program (e.g., developing mission statements, changing policies and written materials) so that anti-bias values would be more likely to endure a change in leadership.

Debbie also recognizes that even when an anti-bias mission and systems are in place, nothing is permanent:

New program leaders may work in a different style and still support the anti-bias mission itself. If the staff and families have a deep commitment to anti-bias values, then there is hope that they will advocate for the anti-bias mission, collaborate with a new leader, and continue to grow in their practice. The values have become a part of who the teachers are as people and professionals. The student teachers have carried an anti-bias perspective into their own practice as they move into the field. For myself, I see colleagues and families that I have worked with over the years continue to pass on and transmit anti-bias values in whatever they do and wherever they go. This is a legacy of effective leadership.

CARRY ON THE MOVEMENT FOR CHANGE: A FEW WORDS FROM LOUISE

Education for social justice and equity has a long history in the United States. When an enslaved African taught others to read, he was engaging in social justice and equity work, even though it was an act that brought horrific punishment if caught. When teachers set up Freedom Schools in the South during the civil rights movement, or taught children in the internment camps where Japanese Americans were unjustifiably imprisoned during World War II, they were doing social justice and equity education. When they engage with children of migrant workers or undocumented immigrant children, they also carry on the tradition of providing education to all.

Engaging in antibias education was, for me, an integral part of the professional ethics I accepted when I became an early childhood educator—to nurture all children's development and learning. When I began working as an adult pre-and-in-service educator, I understood that promise to mean learning how to enable other teachers to carry out this fundamental ethic of our profession. As simple and as complex as that. Like Debbie and John, I also cannot imagine not doing anti-bias work. Anti-bias endeavors are part of a proud educational tradition—one that continues to seek to make the dream of justice and equality for all a reality. It happens day by day, and calls on our best teaching, relationship, and leadership skills. Perhaps the most vital lesson of my long experience is that no one does social justice and change work alone. This is just as true for being an anti-bias educator. It assuredly takes a network of supportive colleagues with whom we can be totally honest, share both failures and successes, and grow personally and professionally.

Early childhood anti-bias educators sow seeds and nurture their growth. Sometimes we are able to see these seeds grow before us; other times they come to fruition after we can no longer see them. There are now many anti-bias seed planters and growers in the USA and in many countries around the world. That is what keeps us carrying on. We agree with social justice activist Pete Seeger's pithy statement to a reporter in 2008, who asked Pete to reflect on his legacy. He said,

Can't prove a damn thing, but I look upon myself as old grandpa. There's not dozens of people now doing what I try to do, not hundreds, but literally thousands. The idea of using music to try to get the world together is now all over the place. (Talbott & Hill, 2014, p. 3)

It is up to all of us to keep anti-bias education expanding and getting better. As Carol Brunson Day (2010) wrote in her foreword to *Anti-Bias Education for Young Children and Ourselves*, "And should you choose to fully engage in the journey, your reward will be a renewed sense of hope that by your own hand, things really can change" (p. vi).

References

Alinsky, S. D. (1971). *Rules for radicals: A pragmatic primer for realistic radicals.* New York, NY: Random House.

Allen, J. (2007). *Creating welcoming schools: A practical guide to home–school partnerships with diverse families.* New York, NY: Teachers College Press.

Alliance for Childhood. (2010). Joint statement of early childhood health and education professionals on the common core standards initiative. Retrieved from bit.ly/1A5NoXj

Anderson, M. L., & Collins, P. H. (Eds.). (1997). Shifting the center and reconstructing knowledge. In M. L. Anderson & P. H. Collins (Eds.), *Race, class and gender: An anthology* (3rd ed.). Belmont, CA: Wadsworth/Thomson Learning.

Beonson, P., & Merryman, A. (2009, September 14). See baby discriminate. *Newsweek*, pp. 53–59.

Berger, E. H. (2008). *Parents as partners in education: Families and schools working together* (7th ed.). Upper Saddle River, NJ: Pearson Education.

Bloom, P.J. (1997). Commentary. In S. Kagan & B. Bowman (Eds.), *Leadership in early care and education* (pp. 34–37). Washington, DC: NAEYC.

Bloom, P. J., Hentschel, A., & Bella, J. (2010). *A great place to work: Creating a healthy organizational climate.* Lake Forest, IL: New Horizons.

Boulton, D. (n.d.) The neuroscience of nurturing neurons. [Interview with Jack P. Shonkoff] Retrieved from www.childrenofthecode.org/interviews/shonkoff.htm

Bowman, B. (1997). New directions in higher education. In S. Kagan & B. Bowman (Eds.), *Leadership in early care and education* (pp. 107–114). Washington, DC: NAEYC.

Brown, B. (1998). *Unlearning discrimination in the early years.* Stoke-on-Trent, United Kingdom: Trentham Books.

Brown, B. (2008). *Equality in action: A way forward with persona dolls.* Stoke-on-Trent, United Kingdom: Trentham Books.

Brown, N., & Manning, J. (2000). Core knowledge for directors. In M. Culkin (Ed.), *Managing quality in young children's programs: The leader's role* (pp. 78–96). New York, NY: Teachers College Press.

Carlsson-Paige, N. (2010). How ed policy is hurting early childhood education. Retrieved from www.nancycarlsson-paige.org/articles13.html

Carter, M., & Curtis, D. (1994). *Training teachers: A harvest of theory and practice.* St. Paul, MN: Redleaf Press.

Carter, M., & Curtis, D. (2010). *The visionary director: A handbook for dreaming, organizing, and improvising in your center* (2nd ed.). St. Paul, MN: Redleaf Press.

Chen, D. W., Nimmo, J., & Fraser, H. (2009). Becoming a culturally responsive early childhood educator: A tool to support reflection by teachers embarking on the anti-bias journey. *Multicultural Perspectives, 11*(2), 101–106.

Child Study and Development Center. (2005). *Diversity commitment.* Retrieved from www.chhs.unh.edu/csdc/diversity-commitment

Child Study and Development Center. (2011). *Family handbook.* Retrieved from www.chhs.unh.edu/csdc/family-handbook

Child Study and Development Center. (2013). *Staff handbook.* Unpublished manuscript, Child Study and Development Center, University of New Hampshire, Durham.

Clark, K. B. (1963). *Prejudice and your child* (2nd ed.). Boston, MA: Beacon Press.

Clark, K. B. (1988). Introduction to the Wesleyan University Press Edition. In K. B. Clark, *Prejudice and your child* (2nd rev. ed., pp. xv–xxix). Middletown, CT: Wesleyan University Press.

Clark, K. B., & Clark, M. P. (1947). Racial identification and preference in Negro children. In T. M. Newcomb & E. L. Hartley (Eds.), *Readings in social psychology* (pp. 169–178). New York, NY: Free Press.

Clemens, S. (1988). A Dr. Martin Luther King, Jr. curriculum: Playing the dream. *Young Children, 43*(2), 6–11.

Clifford, R. (1997). Commentary. In S. Kagan & B. Bowman (Eds.), *Leadership in early care and education* (pp. 103–104). Washington, DC: NAEYC.

Copple, C., & Bredekamp, S. (2009). *Developmentally appropriate practice in early childhood programs: Serving children from birth through age 8* (3rd ed.). Washington, DC: NAEYC.

Creaser, B., & Dau, E. M. (Eds.). (1996). *The anti-bias approach in early childhood*. Pymbie, NSW, Australia: Harper Educational Publishers.

Cross, W. E., Jr. (1991). *Shades of black: Diversity in African-American identity*. Philadelphia: Temple University Press.

Day, C. B. (2010). Foreword: A renewed sense of hope. In L. Derman-Sparks & J. O. Edwards, *Anti-bias education for young children and ourselves* (p. iv). Washington, DC: NAEYC.

Defending the Early Years (DEY). (n.d.). About Defending the Early Years, Retrieved from dey-project.org/about

Derman-Sparks, L. (2011, May 20). *Putting visions into practice: Reflections from an anti-bias educator*. Keynote presentation for Building Peaceable Communities: The Power of Early Childhood, The Global Learning Initiative on Children and Ethnic Diversity Conference, Amsterdam, The Netherlands.

Derman-Sparks, L. (2013a). Developing culturally responsive caregiving practices: Acknowledge, ask, and adapt. In E. A. Virmani & P. L. Mangione (Eds.), *Infant/toddler caregiving: A guide to culturally sensitive care* (2nd ed., pp. 68–94). Sacramento, CA: California Department of Education.

Derman-Sparks, L. (2013b, January 10, 2013). An updated guide for selecting anti-bias children's books [Blog post]. bbpbooks.teachingforchange.org/2013-guide-anti-bias-childrens-books

Derman-Sparks, L., & Edwards, J. O. (2010). *Anti-bias education for young children and ourselves*. Washington, DC: NAEYC.

Derman-Sparks, L., & Phillips, C. B. (1997). *Teaching/learning anti-racism: A developmental approach*. New York, NY: Teachers College Press.

Derman-Sparks, L., & Ramsey, P. G. (with Edwards, J. O.). (2011). *What if all the kids are White? Anti-Bias/multicultural education for young children and families* (2nd ed.). New York, NY: Teachers College Press.

Dunst, C. J., & Trivette, C. M. (2012). Moderators of the effectiveness of adult learning method practices. *Journal of Social Sciences, 8,* 143–148.

Ehrenreich, B. (2011). *Nickel and dimed: On (not) getting by in America* (10th anniversary ed.). New York, NY: Picador.

Eliot–Pearson Children's School. (n.d.). FAQs about anti-bias education at the Eliot Pearson Children's School. In *About the School*. Retrieved from ase.tufts.edu/epcs/aboutAnti-Bias.asp

Espinosa, L. (1997). Personal dimensions of leadership. In S. Kagan & B. Bowman (Eds.), *Leadership in early care and education* (pp. 97–104). Washington, DC: NAEYC.

Feeney, S. & Freeman, N. (2014, March). Standardized testing in kindergarten. *Young Children, 69*(1), 84–88.

Freire, P. (1970). *Pedagogy of the oppressed.* New York, NY: Seabury Press.

Freire, P. (1985). Reading the world and reading the word: An interview with Paulo Freire. *Language Arts, 62*(1), 15–21.

Garcia, E. (2010). *Young English language learners: Current research and emerging directions for practice and policy.* New York, NY: Teachers College Press.

González, N., Moll, L., & Amanti, C. (2005). *Funds of knowledge: Theorizing practices in households, communities, and classrooms.* Mahwah, NJ: Lawrence Erlbaum.

Gonzalez-Mena, J. (2012). *Child, family, and community: Family-centered early care and education* (6th ed.). Boston, MA: Pearson.

Goodman, M. E. (1952). *Race awareness in young children.* Cambridge, MA: Addison-Wesley.

Greenman, J. (1995). Of culture and a sense of place. *Child Care Information Exchange, 101,* 36–38.

Hard, L., Press, F., & Gibson, M. (2013). 'Doing' social justice in early childhood: The potential of leadership. *Contemporary Issues in Early Childhood, 14*(4), 324–334.

Harms, T., Clifford, R. , & Cryer, D. (2005). *Early childhood environment rating scale (ECERS-R).* (rev. ed.) New York: Teachers College Press

Helmer, S., & Eddy, C. (2012). *Look at me when I talk to you, EAL learners in non-EAL classrooms.* Don Mills, Ontario, Canada: Pippin Publishing.

Helms, J. E. (1993). *Black and white racial identity.* New York, NY: Praeger.

Helms, J. E. (1995). An update of Helms' white and people of color racial identity models. In J. Ponterotto, J. Casas, C. Suzuki, & C. Alexander (Eds.), *Handbook of multicultural counseling* (pp. 189–198). Thousand Oaks, CA: Sage.

Hernandez, R. P. (2011, Summer). Transforming for diversity. The Director's Link, (The McCormick Center for Early Childhood Leadership), pp. 1–2., Retrieved from www.the-registry. org/Portals/0/Documents/Credentials/Administrator/Documents/Transforming%20 for%20Diversity%20NLU.pdf

Hirschfeld, A. (2008). Children developing conceptions of race. In S. M. Quintana & C. McKown (Eds.), *Handbook of race, racism and the developing child* (pp. 37–54). Hoboken, NJ: Wiley.

Illinois State Board of Education, Division of Early Childhood. (2013). *Illinois early learning standards.* Springfield, IL: Illinois State Board of Education.

Jacobson, T. (2003). *Confronting our discomforts: Clearing the way for anti-bias in early childhood.* Portsmouth, NH: Heinemann.

Jones, E., & Nimmo, J. (1994). *Emergent curriculum.* Washington, DC: NAEYC.

Kagan, S., & Neuman, M. (1997). Conceptual leadership. In S. Kagan & B. Bowman (Eds.), *Leadership in early care and education* (pp. 59–64). Washington, DC: NAEYC.

Karp, S. (2013–2014, Winter). The problems with the Common Core. *Rethinking Schools, 28*(2), 1–10. Retrieved from www.rethinkingschools.org/archive/28_02/28_02karp.shtm

Katz, L.G. (1985). *The nature of professions: Where is early childhood education?* Office of Educational Research and Improvement, Washington, DC. (ERIC Clearinghouse on Elementary and Early Childhood Education, Urbana, Ill. ED 265948)

Katz, L. G. (1993). *Dispositions: Definitions and implications for early childhood practice.* (Perspectives from ERIC/EECE: Monograph series no. 4). ERIC/EECE Archive of Publications and Resource, Catalog No. 211 Retrieved from ceep.crc.uiuc.edu/eecearchive/books/disposit.html

Katz, P. A. (1976). The acquisition of racial attitudes in children. In P. A. Katz (Ed.), *Towards the elimination of racism* (pp. 125–154). New York, NY: Pergamon.

King, M. L., Jr. (1983). *The words of Martin Luther King, Jr.: Selected by Coretta Scott King.* New York, NY: Newmarket Press.

Krechevsky, M., Rivard, M., & Burton, F. R. (2010). Accountability in three realms: Making learning visible inside and outside the classroom. *Theory Into Practice, 49* (1), 64–71.

Kretzmann, J. P., & McKnight, J. L. (1993). *Building communities from the inside out: A path toward finding and mobilizing a community's assets.* Chicago, IL: ACTA.

Kugelmass, J. (2004). *The inclusive school: Sustaining equity and standards.* New York, NY: Teachers College Press.

Kuh, L., Beneke, M., LeeKeenan, D., & Given, H. (in press). Moving beyond anti-bias activities: Supporting the development of anti-bias practice. *Young Children.*

Kurusa, M. (2008). *The streets are free.* Toronto, Canada: Annick Press.

Lane, J. (2008). *Young children and racial justice.* London, United Kingdom: National Children's Bureau.

Lawrence-Lightfoot, S. (2003). *The essential conversation: What parents and teachers can learn from each other.* New York, NY: Ballantine Books.

Lynch, E., & Hanson, M. (Eds.). (2011). *Developing cross-cultural competence* (4th ed.). Baltimore, MD: Brookes.

Mac Naughton, G., & Davis, K. (2009). *"Race" and early childhood education: An international approach to identity, politics, and pedagogy.* New York, NY: Palgrave Macmillan.

McAfee, O., Leong, D., & Bodrova, E. (2004). *Basics of assessment: A primer for early childhood professionals.* Washington, DC: NAEYC.

Mallory, B., & New, R. (1994). *Diversity and developmentally appropriate practices: Challenges for early childhood education.* New York, NY: Teachers College Press.

Miller, E., & Carlsson-Paige, N. (2013, January 29). A tough critique of Common Core on early childhood education. In *The Answer Sheet by Valerie Strauss, Washington Post.* Retrieved from www.washingtonpost.com/blogs/answer-sheet/wp/2013/01/29/a-tough-critique-of-common-core-on-early-childhood-education

Morgan, G. (2000). The director as a key to quality. In M. Culkin (Ed.), *Managing quality in young children's programs: The leader's role* (pp. 40–58). New York, NY: Teachers College Press.

Morgan, H. (2008). A director's lot is not a happy one. In B. Neugebauer & R. Neugebauer (Eds.), *The art of leadership: Managing early childhood organizations* (pp. 41–43). Redmond, WA: Exchange Press.

Morris, A. (1993). *Bread, bread, bread.* New York, NY: Harper & Collins.

Murray, C., & Urban, M. (2012). *Diversity and equity in early childhood: An Irish perspective.* Dublin, Ireland: Gill & Macmillan.

National Association for the Education of Young Children (NAEYC). (n.d.). TORCH (The Online Resources Center Headquarters). In *NAEYC Accreditation.* Retrieved from www.naeyc.org/academy/primary/torch

National Association for the Education of Young Children (NAEYC). (1995). *Responding to linguistic and cultural diversity: Recommendations for effective early childhood education: A position statement of the National Association for the Education of Young Children.* Washington, DC: Author.

National Association for the Education of Young Children (NAEYC). (2011). *Code of ethical conduct and statement of commitment: A position statement of the National Association for the Education of Young Children* (revised ed.). Washington, DC: Author.

National Association for the Education of Young Children (NAEYC). (2007). *Early childhood program standards and accreditation criteria: The mark of quality in early childhood education* (rev. ed.). Washington, DC: Author.

National Association for the Education of Young Children (NAEYC) & National Association of Early Childhood Specialists in State Departments of Education (NAECS/SDE). (2002). *Early learning standards: Celebrating the conditions for success:* A joint position statement. Washington, DC: Authors.

National Association for the Education of Young Children (NAEYC) & National Association of Early Childhood Specialists in State Departments of Education (NAECS/SDE). (2003). *Early childhood curriculum, assessment, and program evaluation: Building an effective, accountable system in programs for children birth through age 8.* A joint position statement. Washington, DC: Authors.

National Governors Association Center for Best Practices & Council of Chief State School Officers. (2010). *Common Core State Standards*. Washington, DC: Authors.

Neugebauer, R. (2000). What is management ability? In M. Culkin (Ed.), *Managing quality in young children's programs: The leader's role* (pp. 97–111). New York, NY: Teachers College Press.

Neugebauer, R. (2008). Are you an effective leader? In B. & R. Neugebauer (Eds.), *The art of leadership: Managing early childhood organizations* (pp. 4–10). Redmond, WA: Exchange Press.

Nieto, L. (2010). *Beyond inclusion, beyond empowerment: A developmental strategy to liberate everyone*. Olympia, WA: Cuetzpalin.

Office of Head Start. (2010). *The head start child development and early learning framework*. Retrieved from eclkc.ohs.acf.hhs.gov/hslc/sr/approach/cdelf

Olatunji, C. (1998). Toward a model of cross-cultural group process and development. In S. Cronin, L. Derman-Sparks, S. Henry, C. Olatunji, & S. York (Eds.), *Future vision, present work: Learning from the culturally relevant anti-bias leadership project* (pp. 92–109). St. Paul, MN: Redleaf Press.

Palmer, P. J. (1997). *The courage to teach*. San Francisco: Jossey-Bass.

Park, C., LeeKeenan, D., & Given, H. (in press). A family, a fire, and a framework: Emotions in an anti-bias school community. In S. Madrid, D. Fernie, & R. Kantor (Eds.), *Framing the emotional worlds of the early childhood classroom*. New York, NY: Routledge Press.

Pelo, A., & Davidson, F. (2000). *That's not fair: A teacher's guide to activism with young children*. St. Paul, MN: Redleaf Press.

Phillips, C. B. (1995). Culture: A process that empowers. In P. Mangione (Ed.), *A guide to culturally sensitive care* (pp. 2–9). Sacramento, CA: WestEd and California Department of Education.

Ramsey, P. (2004). *Teaching and learning in a diverse world* (3rd ed.). New York, NY: Teachers College Press.

Ray, A., Bowman, B., & Robbins, J. (2006, April). *Preparing early childhood teachers to successfully educate all children: The contribution of four-year undergraduate teacher preparation programs* (Report to the Foundation for Child Development). Chicago, IL: Erikson Institute.

School Reform Initiative (SRI). (2014a). *Diversity rounds*. Retrieved from schoolreforminitiative.org/doc/diversity_rounds.pdf

School Reform Initiative (SRI). (2014b). *Four "A"s text protocol*. Retrieved from schoolreforminitiative.org/doc/4_a_text.pdf

Scott-Little, C., Lesko, J., Martella, J., & Milburn, P. (2007). Early learning standards: Results from a national survey to document trends in state-level policies and practices. *Early Childhood Research and Practice, 9*(1). Retrieved from ecrp.uiuc.edu/v9n1/little.html

Shapiro, I. (2002). *Training for racial equity and inclusion: A guide to selected programs*. Washington, DC: Aspen Institute.

Snow, C.E., & Hemel, S.B. (Eds.). (2008). *Early childhood assessment: Why, what and how*. A report of the National Research Council. Washington, DC: National Academies Press.

Study: White and black children biased toward lighter skin. (2010, May 14). Retrieved from http://www.cnn.com/2010/US/05/13/doll.study/index.html

Sylva, K., Siraj-Blatchford, I., & Taggart, B. (2011). *ECERS-E: The four curricular subscales extension to the Early Environment Rating Scaled (ECERS-R)* (4th ed.). New York, NY: Teachers College Press.

Talbott, C., & Hill, M. (2014). Folk Singer, Activist Pete Seeger Dies in NY. *U-T San Diego*. Retrieved from www.utsandiego.com/news/2014/Jan/27/folk-singer-activist-pete-seeger-dies-in-ny/?#article-copy

Tatum, B. D. (1992). Talking about race, learning about racism: The application of racial identity development theory in the classroom. *Harvard Educational Review, 62*(1), 1–24.

Tatum, B. D. (1994). Teaching white students about racism: The search for white allies and the restoration of hope. *Teachers College Record, 95*, 462–476.

Tatum, B. D. (1997). *"Why are all the black kids sitting together in the cafeteria?" and other conversations about race*. New York, NY: Basic Books.

Teaching Tolerance & Scharf, A.. (2013). *Critical practices for anti-bias education*. Retrieved from www.tolerance.org/sites/default/files/general/PDA Critical Practices.pdf

Trager, H., & Radke Yarrow, M. (1952). *They learn what they live: Prejudice in young children*. New York, NY: Harper & Brothers.

UNICEF. (1990). *Fact sheet: A summary of the rights under the Convention on the Rights of the Child.* New York, NY: UN General Assembly. Retrieved from www.unicef.org/crc/files/Rights_overview.pdf

U.S. Census Bureau (2012, October 9). School enrollment in the United States: 2011 [Press release]. Retrieved from www.census.gov/newsroom/releases/archives/education/cb12-tps57.html

Van Ausdale, D., & Feagin, J. R. (2001). *The first R: How children learn race and racism*. Lanham, MD: Rowman & Littlefield.

Van Keulen, A.(Ed.). (2004). *Young children aren't biased, are they?! : How to handle diversity in early childhood education and school*. Amsterdam, The Netherlands: SWP.

VanderVen, K. (2000). Capturing the breadth and depth of the job: The administrator as influential leader in a complex world. In M. Culkin (Ed.), *Managing quality in young children's programs: The leader's role* (pp. 112–128). New York, NY: Teachers College Press.

Virmani, E. A., & Mangione, P. L. (Eds.). (2013). *Infant/toddler caregiving: A guide to culturally sensitive care* (2nd ed.). Sacramento, CA: California Department of Education.

Wallace, B. (1999). Seeking wholeness. In C. Alvarado, L. Derman-Sparks, & P. G. Ramsey (Eds.), *In our own way: How anti-bias work shapes our lives* (pp. 131–156). St. Paul, MN: Redleaf Press.

Washington, V. (1997). Commentary on Kagan and Neuman. In S. Kagan & B. Bowman (Eds.), *Leadership in early care and education* (pp. 65–66). Washington, DC: NAEYC.

Weingarten, R., & Carlsson-Paige, N. (2013, November 17). Early learning: This is not a test. *New York Times*. Retrieved from www.aft.org/newspubs/press/nytimes/column111713.cfm

Whitney, T. (2002). *Kids like us: Using persona dolls in the classroom*. St. Paul, MN: Redleaf Press.

Wijeyesinghe, C., & Jackson, B., III. (2012). *New perspectives on racial identity development: Integrating emerging frameworks* (2nd ed.). New York, NY: New York University Press.

Wolpert, E. (1996). *Strategies for staff working together with parents and family members*. Unpublished manuscript.

York, S. (2003). *Roots and wings: Affirming culture in early childhood programs* (Rev. ed.). St. Paul, MN: Redleaf Press.

Zeece, P. D. (2008). Power lines: The use and abuse of power in child care programming. In B. Neugebauer & R. Neugebauer (Eds.), *The art of leadership: Managing early childhood organizations* (pp. 25–29). Redmond, WA: Exchange Press.

Index

Adult anti-bias development, 13–19,
  44–45, 91–102
  adult learning goals in, 14–15
  committing to anti-bias education
    framework, 18, 61–69
  community of anti-bias learners
    in, 27–28, 54–61, 99–102
  facilitating educators' work with
    families, 102–108
  life-long learning in, 69
  phases of, 15–18
  professional development
    programs, 30–31, 91–102,
    156–157
  professional learning
    communities in, 98–102
  readiness for anti-bias change
    and, 44–45
  social identity in, 14
African Americans
  civil rights movement, 21, 97–98,
    165
  identity development of, 14
  skin color and, 5, 10
  slavery and, 165
Alinsky, Saul D., 109
Allen, J., 71
Alliance for Childhood, 156
Allies for change, 45–49, 87–89
  ally, defined, 45
  characteristics of, 46
  ECCE colleagues, 47–48
  family, 47, 87–89
  staff, 46
Amanti, C., 71
Amirault, Chris, 28
Anderson, M. L., 12
Annual Family Survey, 144–145
Annual performance assessment, in
    documenting educator change,
    138–139
Anti-bias change. *See also* Anti-bias
    education (ABE)
  allies for, 45–49, 87–89
  assessing. *See* Learning
    assessment tools; Program
    assessment tools
  of children, 139–141
  documenting. *See* Documentation
  impact of, 164–165

indicators in classroom, 134–136
indicators of leader change,
  131–132
planning for. *See* Planning for
  anti-bias change
readiness for, 42–46
recognizing complexity of, 130
recognizing response to, 12–13
resistance to, 17, 44
stakeholders in, 37–39
top-down and bubble-up,
  162–163
Anti-Bias Curriculum (Derman-
  Sparks), 7–8
Anti-Bias Curriculum Task Force,
  Pacific Oaks College and
  Children's School, 7–8
Anti-bias early childhood care and
  education (ECCE) programs
  best practices in, 23–32
  children's identity development
    in, 21–22
  contested grounds for, 19–22
  development theories and
    practice, 20–21
  extent of use, 22
  history of early childhood care
    and education programs
    (ECCE), 20
  leaders of, 1. *See also* Anti-bias
    leaders
  learning assessment tools,
    147–152
  program assessment tools, 94,
    138–139, 147–150, 152–154
  role of early childhood care and
    education, 20
Anti-bias education (ABE)
  adult. *See* Adult anti-bias
    development; Anti-bias
    educators; Anti-bias leaders
  anti-bias vision and mission in,
    9–10, 22, 25, 63–66, 143
  becoming, 11–13
  commitment to equity in, 9, 18
  contested grounds for, 19–22
  core goals of, 10–11, 92, 139–141,
    155–156
  in daily curriculum, 92–95
  defined, 3

denial of need for, 16, 44, 63
early childhood care and
  education (ECCE). *See* Anti-
  bias early childhood care and
  education (ECCE) programs
educators in. *See* Anti-bias
  educators; Anti-bias leaders
extent of use, 22
framework for. *See* Anti-bias
  education framework
as norm, 18–19
resistance to, 17, 44
response to change in, 12–13
reviewing, 9–10
teachers in. *See* Anti-bias
  educators; Anti-bias leaders
Anti-Bias Education Forum and
  Exhibit, 145
*Anti-Bias Education for Young Children
  and Ourselves* (Derman-Sparks
  & Edwards), 59, 60–61, 63, 165
Anti-bias education framework, 18,
  61–69
  articulating anti-bias mission
    statement, 63–66
  becoming an anti-bias educator,
    63
  developing critical eye about
    learning environment, 67–69
  introducing anti-bias education,
    61–63
  life-long learning in, 69
  setting anti-bias goals, 66–67
Anti-bias educators, 53–69
  anti-bias education framework
    for, 61–69
  community-building activities,
    56–61
  community of learners approach
    for, 27–28, 54–61, 99–102
  documenting change in, 136–139
  indicators of change in
    classroom, 134–136
  professional development of,
    91–102
  readiness for anti-bias change,
    44–45
  setting individual educator goals,
    67, 68
  as stakeholders in anti-bias

About the Authors

Louise Derman-Sparks has worked for over 50 years on issues of diversity and social justice as a preschool teacher at the Perry Preschool Project, child-care center director, human development faculty member at Pacific Oaks College, and activist. She is author and coauthor of several books, including *Anti-Bias Education for Young Children and Ourselves*, and *What if All the Kids are White? Anti-Bias/Multicultural Education for Young Children and Families*, and of numerous articles. She speaks, conducts workshops, and consults on anti-bias education with children and adults throughout the United States and internationally. Louise is now retired as a professor emerita.

Debbie LeeKeenan is a visiting professor of Early Childhood Education at Lesley University in Cambridge, MA. She was director of the Eliot–Pearson Children's School at Tufts University from 1996 to 2013. In addition to teaching in the Eliot–Pearson Department of Child Study and Human Development at Tufts University in Medford, Massachusetts, she has been a member of the early childhood faculty at the University of Massachusetts in Amherst. She consults widely and is a published coauthor of numerous articles and book chapters. She holds a master's degree in education from the University of New Mexico. She is a former preschool and elementary school teacher.

John Nimmo is an early childhood consultant and teacher educator. From 2003 to 2013, he was Executive Director of the Child Study and Development Center and Associate Professor of Human Development and Family Studies at the University of New Hampshire. In addition to presenting nationally and internationally for almost 30 years, he has been a visiting scholar at universities in Ghana and Australia. Formerly, he was core faculty in teacher education and human development at Pacific Oaks College Northwest in Seattle. His publications include *Emergent Curriculum* (with Elizabeth Jones), as well as many chapters and articles. He holds a doctorate from the University of Massachusetts in Amherst and was previously an early childhood and elementary teacher in his first home of Australia and in the United States.